Turning the Page is not a fictional st
account of calligrapher and painter A
surrender to Guruji, and how faith h̶e̶l̶p̶e̶d̶ ̶h̶e̶r̶ ̶t̶r̶i̶u̶m̶p̶h over the
most testing decades of her life.

In our day-to-day lives, we come across several people
completely stressed out over situations far less challenging than
what Anita had to endure at multiple levels. The absence of
faith only compounds their lives, making them vulnerable to the
turbulences of the journey of life. However, the power and magic
of faith lie dormant in each of us and need but the right touchstone
to shine through and lead us to peace, love and compassion.

Anita found her touchstone and anchor in Guruji, and
thereafter, a new life. Undoubtedly, her experiences shall inspire
several others to embrace Guruji's divine light that leads us away
from darkness and despair to our own inner radiance.

RP Sharma, Guruji's devotee

Turning the Page

Anita Kumar

Om Books International

Reprinted in 2018
Om **Books International**

Corporate & Editorial Office
A-12, Sector 64, Noida 201 301
Uttar Pradesh, India
Phone: +91 120 477 4100
Email: editorial@ombooks.com
Website: www.ombooksinternational.com

Sales Office
4379/4B, Prakash House, Ansari Road
Darya Ganj, New Delhi 110 002, India
Phone: +91 11 2326 3363, 2326 5303
Fax: +91 11 2327 8091
Email: sales@ombooks.com
Website: www.ombooks.com

ISBN: 978-93-81607-75-6

10 9 8 7 6 5 4 3 2

Printed at Thomson Press, India

Contents

This book is dedicated
with love to
My mother and my father
My daughters, Anishka and Sonakshi
and above all
To my Guruji

Guruji

God has planned happiness for each one of us at the right time;
it is only that He does not share His calendar with us…

Motivational quote

Coming to Guruji for the first time was an invitation to meet myself at a deeper level. I could have either ignored the invitation or discredited the experience after my first encounter with Him but the longing for my own truth pulled me with an irresistible force. I met God in the human form, God who sat before me to redeem me and to show me the way in case I was interested. He had the answers to many of my questions on life and He had the solutions to many of my problems but was I prepared to give Him the one thing He asked of me?

'Surrender.'

It's a big word and I knew the meaning was even bigger! With my endless desires, Guruji knew that I hadn't quite captured the essence of the word but what He also knew is that I had fallen in love with the divine Himself.

Without the embrace of my Guru's love, compassion and grace, I would undoubtedly be walking in life's wilderness, wondering what my soul is and if I had one then, what its true purpose was? It is not only mine but every individual's perennial search of 'who am I?' that draws us towards light.

I said yes to the invitation and it is that which lead to an awakening. An awakening from what? Was I asleep like perhaps most people? In reality, most of us do live our lives on autopilot and some of us are on the treadmill of life with no time to stop and reflect on what truly matters.

I awakened from my ignorance. I was shaken out of the recurrent patterns of my karma. I attracted the same situations to which I was giving the same responses and reactions that kept me trapped in a web of my behaviour patterns.

Who can break many lifetimes of your karma besides the True One, the Supreme and the Merciful One who falls in love with you despite your many defects? I fell in love with Guruji but at first because I knew I would benefit greatly from doing so! My love was conditional and it wanted to receive far more than it wanted to give, if at all! My mind's wants may or may not have been met but I know without a shadow of doubt that my soul's needs were being met without my realising, as my mind was far too busy counting the wants it so longed for!

Life, whether we know it or not, whether we even believe it or not, is all about the journey of the soul and whatever experiences we go through in life are all eventually for the growth of the soul. I believe we seal our own fate by attracting certain situations and people in order not to sail away from difficulties but to come ashore to our own truth through the rough seas. This realisation is not possible when we are either in or even close to the situation. After taking a step back, we have a broader view of the difficulties

projected before us and after the storm has passed and we

have learnt and internalised the lesson, we are stronger, more self-confident and self-assured. Hence, in the larger scheme of things, the people we attract into our lives are merely instruments for our own spiritual evolution.

I am eternally grateful, literally, for all the highs and lows with all the people and events in my life as they are what fuelled my search for an even path, a road that may be bumpy at times but on attaining an inner composure, is now travelled on without turbulence.

After 14 years of my perplexing, puzzling and often pleasurable journey with Guruji, my love for Him has now grown to be unconditional. I seldom question Him and most often allow the answers to my past karmas to unfold with a kind of acceptance that accompanies patience. I try not to indulge in activities that take me off course but when I do, I quickly acknowledge it to Him with a tiny prayer: 'Dear Guruji, please allow me to live in accordance with your laws ALL the time but if I slip now and then, which I know I do more often than I care to confess, then give me the sense not to do it again!'

A mere mortal meets his or her most adored star like Julia Roberts or Brad Pitt. The heart skips a beat or two and then screams in mindless thrill. The body trembles in manic excitement while the juices flow ceaselessly. The balance is lost somewhere in those few transient moments. The experience is shared exultantly with every friend and stranger you come across and you make it a point to perhaps lay it on thick by telling them that your idol called you beautiful, asked you out on a date and even kissed your cheek which you'll never care to wash as long as you live! The euphoria lasts briefly until the mind again seeks yet another excitement to entertain it and in the interim period, feels empty, edgy and extremely restless.

When my search for my own truth began, my restlessness abated. On my every meeting with Guruji, I felt like I was falling in love all over again, coming face to face with my greatest idol.

I loved Him when He was in the physical body and I love Him now. However, I still live with this uncertainty of whether or not I am completely worthy of His love but I am working on that. Someday I know that my frequency will rise to a level where I will be a medium of His expression and purpose. That is my prayer and affirmation.

I have memories of Him holding my hand and me kissing his, looking into His eyes as one would into a loved one's, and then, with a momentary fixed gaze, assimilating that ultimate love that melted me for a milli-second or two and added a radiance to my face. On leaving Him, there would always be a mild regret and sadness till our next encounter.

Today I live with that feeling of love and being loved at most times sans the restlessness and urge to kiss His hand and to place it on both my eyes. I feel His presence in my life and even though I cannot see Him with my naked eyes, my soul sees and feels Him and realises the magnitude of His greatness.

Visiting His temple, being with my Guru's family with whom I share a deep kinship, sharing my satsangs (spiritual gatherings) and living Him as much as I can in my human capacity, is all meditation for my soul and medication for my body. After being healed by Guruji on a number of levels, my consciousness began to expand and I began to benefit from each of my life's experience with greater awareness, be it interacting with friends or strangers, travelling, painting, teaching, socialising, or even savouring the solitary moments when Guruji accompanies me!

Guruji taught me a simple truth that it is not about the events or the people that we attract into our lives that define us, as they are each an integral part of our karma but it is how we handle them and with what attitude that determine their ultimate effect on us. The enduring effect of any ordeal is determined largely on how positive or how negative our attitudes are and how resilient our spirit is. Difficulties come into our lives not to knock us down or diminish us. On the contrary, they come for the expansion of our consciousness and to enable us to live a life that transforms our own and others' for the better. What the human personality regards as an ordeal may be a good deal for the soul and its spiritual evolution. Ordeals and difficulties take us from the personal to the universal but then that is for the wise to accept and those who are otherwise, to reject!

Time and again we are told each time a crisis befalls us, 'It's fate.' 'Maybe it was your karma.' 'God is just testing you.' 'You know these things can't be explained but patience is a virtue.' 'The darkest night is that before dawn, so hang in there.' 'I know you are devastated now but time heals.' 'Think positive and don't dwell on the negative.' 'These things are not in our hands as it's all part of the divine plan.' 'Let go and let God.' 'The bad always happens to the good.' 'Aww, you will come out stronger from this, that or the other, or whatever!'

I was even advised to go feed the poor as I must have had some karmic debt I needed to clear. Someone suggested that I council women from broken homes as by doing so, my own home, that is, my marriage, may be saved,.

Words of reassurance when things have gone terribly wrong in our lives are many. Perhaps partially or totally those afore-mentioned sentences in quotes are true, but I know one truth is absolute: with the impartial blessings of the Enlightened One in the form of a guru or an avatar, the karma that each one is undergoing is cleansed with a higher awareness. The guru reduces the intensity and the duration of the karma so that we are able to live our lives with grace and gratitude.

Every difficult phase that I may go through now, I view it very differently from the way I used to. Every seemingly confining and constricting space is actually a gateway to realisation and expansion. A life without cause is a life without effect.

With every breath I take, I say 'Thank you' to my dear Guruji who has proven time and again, even when doubt clouds my senses, that He is my father, mother, brother and my best friend.

I will now let you, Guruji, do your work while I do mine.

A resonant and reverent thank you.

Acknowledgements

Before my father passed on, he looked me in the eye and said, 'I'm still waiting for you to write your book.' Did he know that there were chapters and verses of my experiences waiting to shared with the world, to encourage, inspire and render hope to every reader? I knew I had to write, particularly after he left this world and I had to rebuild mine.

Writing about my journey with Guruji and my recovery from my divorce is to crystallise the concept and theory of karma, so clearly illustrated in my own life. Being able to transcend the difficult karmas was possible only with the blessings of the Supreme One.

I have been blessed with carefully chosen friends and more well-wishers than I can count. Love envelopes my world and it was that love that encouraged me to write this book.

I thank:

My father Mr KL Kumar who knew that I would;

My mother Mrs Shukla Kumar for always being there with her unconditional love;

My daughters Anishka and Sonakshi who knew that I could;

My friends for asking me if that book of mine was still being worked on and if I slowed down, for speeding me up. Rahul, Seema, Sumi, Anisha, Bonny, and everyone else whom I have failed to mention, just know that I couldn't have done it without your untiring support;

My brothers Rajan, Ajay, Sanjay and Sanjeev who have always known that there was a book within me;

My sisters-in-law Rittu, Selena and Kajal who have been my sisters all along;

My cousins Meenu, Hapu, and, most importantly, Priya who even read the entire book and loved it before I considered publishing it;

My Guru family, particularly Mr RP Sharma, for believing in the book and taking it forward.

Above all, I thank the one who has still kept me on planet earth to give my most incredible experiences the expression that hopefully will encourage you, the reader, to follow the path of self-realisation.

Thank you for all eternity, Guruji.

Aum Aum Aum
Om Namah Shivay Shivji Sada Sahay
Om Namah Shivay Guruji Sada Sahay

Preface

We are what our deep driving desire is
As our desire is, so is our will
As our will is, so is our deed
As our deed is, so is our destiny.

Hindu scriptures

Never stop! Go on believing with all that you have got! Push, push and push till you reach the top! Unless faith is unstoppable, it will falter or fall along the way. Faith has a mind of its own, so it can simply waver or weaken. Faith is what makes the world go round and mine began with the power of faith and nothing but that. I came to the edge and I challenged all the forces of the universe, seen and unseen, to grant me my birthright, my freedom. There came a point of do or die when my faith became as insurmountable as my life hurdles. Faith is anything but gentle or genial. Faith is assertive, aggressive, adamant, all encompassing, argumentative, and, at times, awkward because faith makes you appear absurd!

I had many unsavoury remarks coming my way: 'The poor girl has lost it, so she is trying to find herself through faith.' 'She has gone through so much, so I guess faith is her solace.' 'Not sure about her Guru but then whatever makes her happy, as at least she didn't succumb to substance abuse!' 'Such things are for the feeble-minded as the strong make their own destiny.'

Invariably on becoming regular at Guruji's ashram and signing up for a lifelong course in 'faith', people at large will ask you if everything is ok with you because if it is, then you wouldn't be so staunch! In the eyes of the world, surrendering yourself to the world of faith is a sign of weakness. 'Life is a party and there's plenty of time before taking "that" path. "That" path is for losers and in today's modern world, who believes in all this anyway? It's all within us so there is really no need to go anywhere!'

Different strokes for different folks but when the canvas of my life changed from grey to rose, I had to paint the rest of my life using only one unfading and unfailing brushstroke. Even there, I am not the doer, He is: My Guru (GU-remover of darkness who takes you into light-RU). Before meeting Him, my life was rootless with my situation being rather ruthless but He came along and steeped me in deep devotion and dedication.

In today's volatile climate, Guruji had stated at the turn of the century, 'I see difficult times ahead. There will be natural calamities, recession, depression and floods of uncertainties, so in this unstable world, the only stability is faith that not only keeps your head above water but enables you to cross the ocean of worldly existence with absolute love, life and laughter. Connect to the divine and disconnect yourselves from the attachment to the illusory, transient pleasures and incessant desires.' People have it all today with all their gadgets and the latest this and that but the essential element is missing in most people's lives. On connecting to Him, I realised that I connected better to the world! I became a happier and healthier individual who viewed and enjoyed life from a new perspective. I ceased to live on the surface sans substance. There was a newfound focus and purpose and that springs only from spirituality synonymous with simplicity, silence and positive surrender. Nam bheej lo (Sow the seed of faith) as the season has arrived.

With the enduring power of faith, my inner landscapes transformed first before my outer ones did. Faith is not a one-stop-shop where you draw all that you want and move on. Faith is an on-going journey that unfolds many truths that lie within us and within the sights and sounds of everyday life. Faith is life-enhancing and those who have risked being labelled a 'loser' will know that through the wonders of faith, they have become absolute winners.

This is an unconventional love story with no ending…

Anita Kumar

Prologue

*A man sooner or later discovers that he is
the master-gardener of his soul, the director of his life.*

Allen James

For the largest part of my nuptial years, I found myself ensnared in the dark room of apathy and inertia after resentfully resigning myself to a debilitating situation. I assumed that there was no way out as it was beyond me to unlock the hidden gallant nature that would liberate me. However, by conceiving of courage as a universal attribute of human nature, it becomes a possibility for every person in deep marital suffering to take charge for a positive turn of events.

I was visibly unhappy and that in itself was a true indicator that my life was in distress. I sat on a sink-or-swim situation and after long and careful deliberation, I rightfully chose not to sink any further.

I chose to turn a different corner, to no longer live in disgrace and dishonour. My primary motivation was my daughters who would have lost respect for me as well as for the institution of marriage had I stayed any longer. My secondary motivation was my own well-being that I scarcely believed in any more. I shamefully admit that sometimes it is far easier to resign yourself to unscrupulous behaviour than to muster up the courage and strength to do what is ethically right for all involved. I resigned to my lot for many years before I realised that I needed to breathe again and surely life on the other side couldn't be worse than my existing one. I needed to take a chance on life and for that I had to rock my boat. After 18 years of living in my discomfort zone, I took my calligraphy pen and in my usual Italic style wrote, *I am happy, I am strong, I am happy,* God knows how many times only to fill many pages for many hours affirming that which needed to be believed and acted on.

Achieving unfeigned happiness after prolonged sadness is a long-drawn process and a conscious choice. Once my reasons for abandoning my marriage were legitimate, I needed to approach my 'life after' very carefully and constructively. My fragile self-image and self-esteem that had hit rock bottom needed serious working on after honestly acknowledging that my marriage too that had hit rock bottom after it had been seriously worked on, needed to be left precisely where it was. It was I who needed to ascend from the bottom and only I would discover the know-how. The recovery pill is different for each individual as there are no one-size-fits-all solutions but amongst many my strongest pill was my spirituality, my inner fortitude and belief that I could redefine my life.

Needless to say, most of us who are in a unhealthy marriage choose to remain there predominantly owing to the fear of the unknown. When we rock our boat, the oceans of emotions lose direction in the turbulence. The storm hits us hard and holding on to faith as the only anchor is like a blind man crossing the road on a traffic-laden road. What I was blind to was my own indomitable force and the protective forces of the universe. I didn't believe that life would meet me with outstretched hands, a warm welcoming smile from my well-wishers with the promise of happiness in the reassuring eyes of my Guru. I was blind to my future but I did consider that with all life's support, my vision would be restored like never before.

The challenge of stepping out of the shadows into the sunlight after a gloomy situation cannot be undermined. I felt that divorce had pushed me back several steps and at first I was eager to rush, to catch up to where I believed I ought to be, until I realised it had to be a step-by-step journey and what I had lost could no longer be found. What can't be cured must be endured and time is one such commodity that once lost cannot be regained. The acceptance of 'what is' rather than, 'what should have been' needed to be embraced. There were many phenomenal occurrences too that contributed to the rebirthing of my mind, body and spirit. One morning, after some years of being officially divorced and working diligently on my recovery, happiness permeated my soul and I developed an intense respect for L-I-F-E (Learning-Institute for a Fearless-Existence.)

The optimistic window through which I view the world today is a result of reconstructing the broken home of my being. To recreate means to first tear down the dilapidated walls of despair and to laboriously lay each rejuvenating brick of self-respect, self-belief, inner fortitude, gratitude, love and hope, as well as tons of other strong building blocks that constitute a sturdy healthy home for the soul to comfortably dwell in. I was not alone, however, in my journey. One never is in extraordinary situations.

1

A Clean Slate

Optimism is a challenge to irony and cynicism.
It's not about passively hoping that things will get better.
Optimism is intrinsic to art making.

Anonymous

Today, I'm proud to state that my life is a clean slate considering it was once soiled with marks and blemishes that I feared would never be wiped away. I was tarnished with every caustic emotion that abraded the very fibres of my being. I had been alienated from my better self and engulfed instead by my bitter self! Life introduced me to myself and I learnt to build a healthy and happy relationship with the one who had gone missing in the dark, dense forest of 18 years.

As a somewhat wise teenager who had the insight and foresight of an old sage, I imbibed the expression 'life begins at 40'. I used to hear myself relate this every so often in my head without understanding why. I would closely observe 40+s and realise that what really begin are the first signs of those much dreaded lines!

I am 44 with a few lines, arguably more wisdom and a divorce!

After 18 years of a tumultuous marriage, 2 years of a turbulent separation that involved a legal battle, I finally broke free from the chains of my deep karma. I was triumphantly granted a divorce. I held the divorce decree like a trophy in both my hands. I held it engagingly like an old friend who had come to grant me a second chance. This was by far the greatest victory of my life and by far the greatest defeat. How I was finally granted the big D is another story that was far from polite and problem-free. Getting a divorce is *never* plain sailing. However, my journey is not about the malady but essentially about the recovery.

In the beginning, it felt like my layers of security had been peeled off placing me in a vulnerable position and victory turned into defeat in a hurry as I saw my journey ahead with uncertainties that knew no bounds. The worst was over without a shadow of doubt but how was I to revive myself with a renewed determination and fresh resolve? The cloud hung over me firmly and determinedly as I felt a sense of isolation and desolation. I was alone on my inner battlefield. My enemy, far greater and stronger than me, needed to be defeated. Inch by inch, it was permeating my being and gripping me callously. My enemy was my fear that had become my second skin, eclipsing my faith awhile, enshrouding me with a darkness that knew no light.

A divorce is an insurmountable undertaking in itself, particularly for an Indian/Asian woman conditioned with values, priorities and attitudes that undermine her own worth. The mental blocks and conditioning are what prevented me from taking the first step into the unknown for the best years of my life but then there never is a right time to divorce. Scores of people asked me 'Why now?' In fact, there were many W's left in people's minds. Why-where-what-when?! I didn't have a perfectly valid answer to give except that divorce is not the first solution to a problem in a marriage. Hence, years go by living with the perennial optimism that things will improve. However, when the marriage is inflicted and infected with deep and incurable abuse, then divorce is the only remedy. I suppose the damage done within the marriage prevented me from having the confidence to do the needful but when that miraculously arrived, I seized its support along with the courage to do what must be done in a long-drawn-out withering situation.

Before courage chose me, I chose to wear the melancholy of my marriage like an uncomfortable old coat and a pair of shoes that never fit! 'Don't throw them away,' I would tell myself. 'They are all you have and you've invested a lot of time and effort in preserving them! Who cares if they are a misfit as long as they look good to the world? Keep up appearances as you have children to think of. Don't fuss, this is life and no one has a perfect fit. If my shoes don't fit, maybe the woman next door is forcefully fitting into a dress she resents only to complete her garb with a well rehearsed smile to conceal her deepest wounds. Happiness is the art of looking happy.' I would repeatedly reason. 'Being an artist you can blend certain shades to create a mood that will enable you to get by. Paint well. So what if the canvas is torn! You can camouflage the flaws dear Anita.' I am certain hundreds, if not thousands, of women I came across in my everyday life in Delhi society had learnt to camouflage their marital blues with brighter hues of life such as burying themselves in social circles or occupying their disturbed minds with retail therapy. They were part of a marital blues association (MBA) and most were trapped in it in the same manner that I was.

One day, however, my positive internal dialogue, creative visualisation and the foundations of my conditioning collapsed hard as the walls of pretense could no longer be upheld: they were clearly covered with webs of lies, deceit, betrayal and maltreatment. The pair of shoes didn't fit and it's not my fault.

3

It's not that my feet have grown over the years or have reduced in size either! I was prepared to confess to my greatest error of errors in taking a pair that I tried so hard to wear with the comfort that would last a lifetime Believe me, I tried and that is why it took 18 years to come face to face with the ugly truth. The smile that the woman next door probably rehearses in front of her mirror to camouflage her pain could not be adopted by me any longer. I wasn't the type to drown myself in ladies' lunches everyday or go shopping needlessly to fill my empty heart and overflowing wardrobe. I frowned implicitly at my misfit shoes, my deep karma, my sealed fate, my orthodox upbringing, my traditional conditioning, my bulging midriff, my fine lines, my dismal life and my failed marriage, as well as at everyone else's marriage! I looked at mine long and hard, straight into its dishonest eyes. Then, with a determination that could move mountains, I walked out abandoning the institution that crippled my self-worth, self-confidence and self-belief.

I was undeniably dejected and undeniably delighted. At that moment of having decided to break free, I had only to be steady and steadfast in moving ahead. I knew there was no looking back as that may mean going back, given my track record. I had gone back more times than I care to recall, out of sheer fear.

I was exactly 40 when I took the leap in the dark. What on earth? Had I determined my own fate as a child? My subconscious had always stated that life begins at 40 but what it forgot to tell me is that so do aches and pains! With an aching body, anguished mind and a forlorn heart, I walked the path that most would shy away from. My daughters, Anishka and Sonakshi, were the balm to soothe me and to walk me through the arduous journey of starting afresh with the unwanted baggage of my past. They, at this point, had divorced trust and had been plagued by the false notion of belonging to a 'broken home'.

I failed in my marriage no doubt but I succeeded in life as 3

years and 7 months after the separation and 1 year and 3 months after the divorce, I started writing on being born again. The twists and turns in each chapter of my recovery and self-discovery are what reinvented me. As a Hindu, I believe in life after death but to actually be reincarnated into a truly happy person after being a deeply unhappy one can only be with the blessings of the Supreme One.

'Onwards and upwards' was my mantra.

2

England

The purpose of life is a life of purpose.

Ralpho Waldo Emerson

I gazed liberally upwards at the expansive sky through the fervent eyes of a 12 year old and onwards at my father's pure paradise of a garden where the tall trees stood regally on the fringes of the verdant lawns that were a pure delight to walk on. England's sky in the month of July is more or less clear blue with shades of pearl white. The strokes are impeccably formed as if God himself has carefully dipped his brush into his palette to create the real-life canvas. I could fix my eyes into the open skies for the rest of my living years while inhaling the clean, crisp fresh air, totally unpolluted that purified my every cell and tissue, filling it with untainted love and joyfulness.

I recall the feeling of elation whilst walking outside in the lush gardens of my father's palatial home that stood majestically in the suburbs of Manchester in a quaint and luscious county of Hale. Our home was a Victorian style one with five sizeable bedrooms with their own attached bathrooms. I shared mine with my younger brother Sanjay whilst Rajan, my eldest, had his own. He also had his study in the attic where he studied diligently and finally scored high to complete his degree in Salford University where Sanjay would head too. Our kitchen was located prominently as we all dined together as a family every evening whilst my mother dutifully served us heartwarming Indian meals with her own sacred hands. My father, a leading garment importer who also had his own cash-and-carry, wouldn't have had it any other way and we knew no different. Every savoury and unsavoury vegetable was to be consumed without question and this is how we cultivated a taste for versatility and flexibility! This spilled over in other non-culinary aspects of my life too where I learnt to accept unsavoury moments without fuss!

Climbers and ramblers covered the white walls of the exterior of our home built in 1901. I revelled in the pristine prettiness of the space that I occupied to think and daydream. I wished for such moments to freeze; they were that soothing.

Nature has its own way of communicating to you; it quietly whispers your destiny and subtly brings you closer to it. I sat on the wooden garden bench and spoke to the God I believed I knew: 'Life feels like an illusion. The laughter of the children next door, the loveliness of this well-manicured garden, the cars driving past, the birds flying through your canvas, my mother cooking the classic aloo gobi (potato and cauliflower) in her kitchen and my father entering the gate in his Rolls Royce are all an illusion. My heart tells me that you are real, so let me meet you and shake hands with you, maybe even give you a warm hug as I would to my truest friend. I know you will never hurt me or will you just to test my strength, my endurance and my faith? I love you wholly and I want to marry you. Will you marry me? Oh but I have a hole in my heart and I have asthma that triggers

7

from time to time and oh my skin! Well I have eczema too, so even though I'm pretty, my skin flares up to make me far from attractive. The inflammation can last for days and sometimes weeks and that can't be such a good thing for my morale.

'Perhaps God you don't exactly find me irresistible and don't fancy being my friend or else you wouldn't have sent me here with bags full of health issues. I spent the best part of my childhood in hospitals and imagine the agony of my parents who were never sure if I would recover from my attacks. You may not be such a fair guy but I do know that you have aroused my curiosity to know what this thing called life is all about. Whilst my brothers and my peers are engaging in vigorous sports, I am sporting the idea of meeting you. Instead of playing with dolls and building doll houses, I have been building my dreams around understanding you and your world.

'God, in all honesty, I'm a wee bit wary of you as grave human suffering like famine in poor nations, religious differences that lead to animosity amongst people you claim to be equal as well as other atrocities across the globe, makes me question your compassion. All the same, I have a soft spot for you. I'm kind of infatuated by you; I just learnt this word recently since some guy gave me the glad eye and my elder brother Rajan said, "He is infatuated by you!" He is protective as is my father. Here in Manchester in the '70s, the roles of men and women, boys and girls are very typical. The standards are set almost immediately on being born. My brothers will typically take over the family business, which is clothing and entertainment whilst I will be expected to build a career in "marriage".

'I'd love to know you over a cup of tea or coffee someday when you have the time. Tea is better since I'm allergic to coffee and spices. In addition, I've been asked to strictly stay clear of alcohol, red meat, preservatives, processed foods, cheese, milk, eggs, seafood and pretty much everything else that's irresistible to the senses (and in very recent years I just added married men to my list after my divorce!) It's doctor's orders. My skin flares up and red blotches envelop my little face but only if I eat any of the forbidden foods or I allow stress to consume me. The latter doesn't happen frequently as I'm a reasonably cheerful gal. I'm only 12 but I have the mind of a sage. I've never played with dolls or dollhouses and I listen to bhajans (devotional songs). I believe my mother is terribly concerned about me as she sees my affection for you grow. On being discharged from hospital, after a ghastly asthma attack, I picked the *Bhagwad Gita* but it's a little violent as the people keep fighting. I haven't been able to grasp the essence of the *Gita* but someday I'll read into it as it is after all our holy book although it is wholly violent!

'Sometimes I feel I'm a misfit in this world as I do lack a sense of belonging. I'm very aloof according to my peers and oh I write poetry, mostly about you and about true love. I also write letters to you practically every day but then you ought to already know that. My diary entry is always addressed to you, "Dear God". Regardless of your opinion of me and my mundane activities like sketching, calligraphy, listening to the renowned Indian playback singers Kishore Kumar and Lata Mangeshkar's duets, watching Hindi videos, top of the pops every Thursday at 7 pm and the hit soap opera, "Dallas" with my father every Saturday; cautiously eating my mother's Indian style rice pudding with almonds; washing the dishes after every evening meal; running hastily up the stairs to my room to escape further domestic chores and writing poems on you, I am in love with you and I'm also probably in love with the notion of "love".

'I do have my reservations about your love for me which makes this love story one-sided. I love you unconditionally and unreservedly (more big words I learnt recently!). Actually, another one of my favorite pastimes is building my vocabulary. I love words and maybe subconsciously, I'm learning more to enable myself to express my love for you more articulately. I'm sure my diction already impresses you!

'I'm 12, but then I've already told you that. I'm a bit of an Alice in Wonderland too but then I'm also pretty intense for my age. Every day, I bow to Guru Nanak's picture as well as Lord Shiva's, Lord Krishna's, Goddess this and Goddess that! My mother has a picture of all of them, just in case! Lord Shiva happens to be my favourite of the trillion and one deities that we Hindus have been blessed with and confused with in the same breath! He is blue but then so am I! I feel blue from time to time while He just looks it all the time! All the pictures stand in our guest room and each of us, from my mother, my father, to my brothers and I, we bow to these pictures every day.

'Rituals? I, for one, never believed in them. The only ritual I observe in our family is my father lighting a tea light candle before the Gods every evening after he returns from work. He is hard working and has made his mark as a leading garment importer in England. He is dynamic and has a very respectable social standing. He is almost an idol to many. Do I believe in idol worship? Never! Actually, that's only partially true as there are a few pop idols that I deeply adore: Phil Collins, Sting, George Michael, Elton John, Stevie Wonder, Madonna and my all-time favorite, Michael Jackson. Oh! And I am also in love with Lord Ganesha, the Elephant God. He is unbelievably cute!

'So coming back to you, do you live here in Manchester, England in my mundane and often difficult life laden with health issues? Are you up in the clear summer skies or are you in my kitchen while I listen to my bhajans and wash the dishes? Are you in my art? Maybe that is the reason for my being so good or so I have been told. "God's gift!" Just listen to me giving you all the credit for my creativity. It's my artistic mind that conjures the images and I give you the credit. I would love to paint someday, too, in the same manner that you paint England's skies. For that I must give you credit. You're an accomplished artist. Your brush strokes are truly outstanding. You must have been practising timelessly. I'm inspired!

'Wherever you are, I'm going to positively meet you face to face one day and ask you a sea of questions. My keen mind wants to know it all as I am drawn to and driven by anything mystic and mysterious.

'A thought just flashed across my mind about you residing in India. You know God, I love India as I love you and maybe someday, I'll go there and meet you. I have read a few parables on Gautam Buddha and his meditations that led to his Enlightenment in India. I love the thought of living out there as well and getting enlightened! I have two brothers, Ajay and Sanjeev, residing there too, and an extended family of cousins. None of them are enlightened but I do kind of fancy the idea for myself although I'm not quite sure what it really means. It's a big word, "Enlightenment". I can definitely extend my menu too, to more than just aloo gobi! They have cooks in abundance as well as loo cleaners, women who dust, sweep and wash all the dirty dishes! I believe they have masseurs too who come home and don't charge the earth as they do here in the West.

I love Hindi movies as you know and our lives also somewhat replicate them! We are one big complicated and fragmented family who unite and become whole every summer break and thanks to them, I get to go to India every year with my brothers which breaks the monotony of our routine of playing video games, snooker and pool. My favourite is table tennis and my father has strategically placed a table in the attic where we play doubles every evening before going down for my mother's cooking and my carefully cut salad that I artistically place on a plate to demonstrate my culinary skills or lack of them!

'My brothers in India attend interesting events and parties whereas here in Manchester, we have the annual Diwali Ball and the New Year's celebration with party poppers and balloons! Oh, and then there are the whistles and hats and maybe the crackers at our dinner table beside our plates. It is very English with a live band that my father and I dance to whilst Rajan dances with my mother. Sanjay simply sits at the table where he vigorously plays with his Rubik's cube and finally falls asleep at the table! At least he won the national competition! He is known as super Sanj in our household as whatever he embarks on, he excels in.

'I'm pretty convinced. The more I reflect on this, the more I am certain that you dwell in India! It's the land of the holy cows, the spectacular temples and all that is mystical and mysterious. I see the magic of you appearing in Hindi movies. The hero, very often, vents his frustration and anger out on you while he's under the influence of alcohol and then after a loud resonance of bell chimes, you respond to him but I'm not angry or frustrated with you yet. There's nothing to be angry about except that you never appear even when my prayers are clear. Maybe I've answered my own question. You reside in India. It's all there and so are you. Marry me!'

The seed of my future was sown in the mind of a 12 year old.

3

New Delhi, India

My garden of flowers is also my garden of thoughts and dreams.
The thoughts grow as freely as the flowers.

Abram L Urban

On the 4th July 1988, precisely 10 years after my extensively naive dialogue with the Almighty, I had my registrar wedding in Manchester to an Indian from India. No it wasn't God! I had the 'Grand' Indian wedding the following day, with a horse but no elephants, and a limousine instead. Then I landed in New Delhi, India after my extensive honeymoon in Vegas, Hawaii, Tokyo, Singapore and Bali. It was exotic and most pleasurable. I would miss my mother's simple cooking but not my subsequent washing the dishes. I no longer had to dash to my room to avoid further domestic chores and, of course, I could have a lavish menu once I reached India with cooks in the kitchen that would not include me! I simply relished the idea of being waited on! What a Queen

Anita! To add to my host of staff, I had my personal maid who served me tea in bed and all my other meals, too, were taken care of by her. Thank goodness for that since the mere thought of entering the kitchen in the sultry temperature of 47°C mortified me.

Call it destiny, fate or karma but I believe it was my search for truth that brought me to the land where my romantic dreams were irrevocably shattered! I resented Delhi almost as soon as I stepped on its soil. The initial euphoria quickly turned sour and acrid. My enduring allergies precipitated further and my temperament, too, was agitated. I encountered the intensity of the heat as well as the rising heat in my marriage that couldn't be cooled off even with the round-the-clock running of air conditioners! My reality here was a far cry from the annual summer vacations spent in Delhi with my brothers. My previous impression of the place being splendid swiftly turned sordid.

I slept during most of my waking hours and stayed awake during the sleeping hours. I simply could not acclimatise to the place or the people, particularly to the person I entrusted my life to. I encountered a total culture shock and a marriage shock. '

I was forlorn as with the passage of time, the veil of illusion lifted and I felt that it wasn't God with whom I'd had the extensive dialogue that lucid summer day in the serenity of my father's garden, my haven till date. It was a trusting conversation in the young gullible mind of a 12 year old. It had led me to believe that some divine being resided here and we would have tea together. There was no dearth of tea and tea-lovers out here and anytime of the day was tea time. It's a way of bonding; tea and snacks and in no time I cultivated a taste for the rich Indian cardamom and ginger tea, which I found soothed my soul. I would sip it at regular intervals throughout the day even in the sweltering heat. Aah tea! I was certain it had come straight from heaven, grown organically in the divine garden. It would tea-se my senses!

I drove in the congested city of Delhi the moment I landed. That was indeed my passport to a glimpse of freedom in my captivity.

14

In 1988, the traffic was more than bearable and very rapidly I learnt the routes. The pollution level was also relatively lower so the green city of Delhi with interesting architecturally styled homes on either side of the roads was a visual delight. Some were palatial and grand whilst others were small and modest, often dilapidated but then that was India for you; always a sharp contrast between the wealthy and the poor. Those days, it was not commonplace to see a woman driving an imported car, that too unaccompanied, so I would attract surprised glances from passersby. Times were very different, still primitive in many ways with a single television channel and a radio station that did far from enliven my senses. Besides the experience of fine dining in luxury hotels, there was not much amusement, so I enrolled myself in a few courses in this and that until I soon started teaching calligraphy, first at home and then in schools. Very soon, I earned the label of the very first 'calligraphy teacher' in Delhi as Anita Bagla, my marital name, and then came to be known in Delhi society as an art-cum-calligraphy teacher. That somewhat gave me a sense of immense personal fulfillment. I worked flexi hours to successfully fulfill the individual requirements of each student primarily to enhance their regular handwriting. Some of them were existing art students at high levels who aimed to incorporate various letterforms to their canvas. They also learnt calligraphic artwork under my experienced guidance. I involved myself wholly with my students' aspirations and it was by engaging myself so deeply that I was able to keep my head above water. A few newspapers and magazines featured my work and interviewed me. Before I left India, I taught many of my students to become teachers and now there are many. I wrote books too on calligraphy before I began painting. Any talent that is first honed and then shared brings a sense of joy into our lives' that is incomparable to all others. Teaching as a profession is most satisfying as you impart knowledge while you affirm your own and there is much to learn from the students who each have their individual creative expression.

I recognised quite early in the marriage that our arrangement was going to be very challenging as the equation with my husband was a poor one particularly with his ever-growing volatile behaviour but I had little choice but to keep the ball rolling. Besides, I believed in the sanctity of marriage and commitment and knew no better as I was programmed that way. Most girls raised in the '80s knew no different and were expected to make it work 'no matter what.' This was the world I had chosen for myself consciously or subconsciously. The soul chooses that which it needs to learn for its growth and evolution.

A pattern which began to develop during my early years in India was the strong bonding with a girlfriend in every chapter of my story. That indeed was a solace and a comfort, to be able to share my grievances and also to find practical solutions to the difficulties I was encountering. A few of those girlfriends are friends to date and I maintain that they have been my pride and pillars of strength all along on my journey. Those who didn't make it to my present were a gift for that time period only and I wrap them up with my good wishes and warmth.

Every three to four months of being here, I would fly back to Manchester on some pretext. This continued for many years including after I had my two most blessed daughters, Anishka and Sonakshi. I would gladly return home. What was high up on my list of things to do was inhaling the fresh, crisp air and gazing up at the clear bluer than blue skies in my father's haven of a garden. I passed this pleasure on to my children who definitely thought Mummy's lost it! Why is she sooooo ecstatic about the air and the sky? We have a sky in India too! The air also exists in India! The blank look on their cute, confused faces would not stop me from inhaling deeper. In the same breath, I would keep them amused in the local park where they would excitedly feed bread to the ducks and care less for the air around them or the skies above their tiny bodies. My girls bonded well with their cousins in Manchester, as by this time, both my brothers Rajan and Sanjay were well settled in their respective marriages and had two children each.

This pattern continued for a while and especially during the changing seasons in Delhi, I needed to speed back to England but I was unable to do so as frequently with my growing girls and responsibilities. Changing seasons were detrimental, as they would unfailingly bring on my asthma attack that would keep me in the ICU for days on end followed by a heavy dose of steroids at home for weeks on end.

My health was fast deteriorating, my self-confidence rapidly diminishing. I had nowhere to turn to for strength. Momentarily, I would find escape in a conversation with my girlfriends who would sympathise before really understanding the abjectness of my marriage. Although I was an eternal optimist, I was not denied the intelligence to recognise that my glass was almost empty and leaking too.

The writing is on the wall usually early on in one's marriage. In clear bold letters, it is scribbled, 'IT'S OVER.' But then the idealistic mind states, again in clear bold letters 'I WILL TRY, TRY AND TRY UNTIL I REALLY DO FAIL.' I was ensnared in my situation, in a tight box that had no key. Through the windows I would gaze up at the open skies. The air was polluted and the skies hazy, a sharp contrast to England's resplendent skies and its refreshingly vibrant air. My asthma attacks became more frequent due to the suffocation I felt in my marriage. I was truly choking and with my every gasp, I hoped it would be my last. I was hopeless and helpless and would often come face to face with the stranger in me only to resent its presence more and more. Where was God? He stated in the holy *Gita* once that his favourite residing place is the human heart. 'OK, no wonder I don't feel him. My heart is in fragments, my soul is in pieces and my mind, I lost that a while ago!'

I was in a loveless marriage, on a terrain where I was fast losing my health, my self- worth, and my self–esteem. I was also losing my dress sense, my desire to socialise, my wish to smile, to be nice and to be alive. Why was I allowing myself to be subjected to such abject misery and heartache? Perhaps I had learned to bear it with a grin that had also turned grim! I had turned into a self-sacrificing martyr and I believed that this was meant to be my lot. The role of a victim seemed to have been assigned to me and I did not know how to re-write my script or to simply get out of the drama. What I would resist would persist, so I was clueless as to how to overcome the existing situation. I truly felt like my predicament was a Berlin Wall with my concrete helplessness holding me captive. The high walls seemed insurmountable, particularly as I felt isolated in my thoughts of never being able to climb over them. A kitchen appliance or a gadget comes with a manual and I've had no issues figuring it out but here there was no manual, neither for 'marriage' nor for 'life'.

The suppression and oppression manifested into more serious issues that would only be diagnosed at a later date. Meanwhile, I kept my head above water by focusing on raising my delicate daughters who were growing up in an unhealthy environment. Thankfully, they were performing well in school and participating in various extra-curricular activities. I loved them dearly and showered my affection on them much more as I believed that the unhealthiness was affecting them on a deep psychological level. I was very protective of them but there was no escaping the environment that they were being raised in. I certainly dreaded them being emotionally and psychologically scarred because of being subjected to my bad marriage. I guess they had their own karma to go through and as a mother, I could only pray for the impact to be minimised. They were studying first in Step By Step nursery, then Amity for a while before I gained admission for both of them in the British School. Their school environment was conducive to their academic and personal growth and with their increasing popularity, they had a strong support system from their friends. I would go in once a week to teach calligraphy as an extra-curricular subject and I would observe the pride in my girls' eyes each time I entered their school. I ardently taught calligraphy and art and conducted workshops in other schools too. Even amidst the insanely unhappy situation where I was fast losing it, there was something invaluable that I managed to retain—oodles of humour that enabled me to brave the elements of the volatility at home and give comic relief to the seriousness of it. The home truth that was otherwise sordid was diluted or lifted with either the comic in me or the philosopher in me. In my solitary moments, I would introspect and examine my situation. 'I loathe myself for being such a coward. I permit the maltreatment and do not stand up for myself. In fact, I sit and anticipate the next ugly encounter. In the face of fear, I cower. Hence, I attract it more. Was this lot pre-ordained? Is it my karma to be subjected to such ill treatment? Has this been predetermined by God? My skin is perpetually flared up and I have gained enormous amounts of weight. To top it up, I can barely breathe even when I'm not having an asthma attack. You could cut the atmosphere of my home with a knife and the stitches that are holding us together too. My sense of who I am is in pieces. I am floating in this dark tunnel of my mind and I am unable to hold a clear, positive conversation with myself. My conversation with myself always seems to be self-deprecatory and disparaging. I am terribly worried about my daughters' emotional well-being. Will they be able to overcome everything that they absorb and assimilate? Do any of us ever get over our childhood memories of the bad encounters with our parents? Aren't our parents' behaviour responsible for the way we view people and situations? Hence, aren't parents our destiny-makers in that sense? The blessed clear open skies of England are a distant and vague dream as my mind is clouded ever more rapidly with polluted thoughts and particles of dust and heat. My skies are further obscured by the mist and haze of my life situation.

19

'Most days, when I am not teaching, I wake up as late as possible so that the days pass by rapidly and swiftly although never smoothly. I choose to remain in my room in the dark because I have no formula on taking charge of my life. I have practically resigned to my destiny with the belief that there are no greener pastures.

'Time is of the essence. I fail to understand how I could possibly be drawing value from this situation but something tells me, possibly my intuition, that, in time, I will see the light. Yes, even in this profoundly dim night, something within me reassures me, reaffirms the idiom that there is always light at the end of every dark tunnel. I marvel at my own unconquerable spirit in spite of it being assaulted repeatedly. Despite being an embittered woman whose once formidable spirit now lies in tatters, there is still an inaudible voice within that endeavours to set my mind at rest. Perhaps it is my unrealistic unfounded faith that waters down the toxins I drink on a daily basis.'

As I was sinking deeper in the abyss of my unhappiness, it was almost impossible to be optimistic. The heaviness I would feel in the centre of my heart chakra (wheel) became a part of me that couldn't be lightened. I was dipping fast and I was far from skilled at camouflaging my pain. My face really was the index of my mind and I was not adept at veiling the truth as my sullen eyes revealed my mental and physical fatigue. I was not even interested in perfecting an image to the outside world that could mask my inner world of fear, insecurity, loneliness and emptiness. 'I am miserable and it's totally justified for me to be this way. This situation is clearly not normal or healthy in any capacity. Hence, I either die a natural death to end this predicament and long-drawn ordeal or gather the courage to come away from this ghastly situation with my beloved girls. At least now I know what love isn't.'

Only something higher, greater and more powerful than the human mind can fathom, needed to intervene to disentangle me from the millions of what seemed like unbreakable threads of my unyielding karma. I was hopeful that a higher energy would see what I was going through and would see me through!

Parents of that era usually had a limited vision of the real situation that their daughters were facing in their marriages. Sometimes, they preferred not to know. Ignorance was bliss.

Time went by and my daughters bonded well with my brothers' children, particularly with Ajay's as, later they too gained admission in British School. The two brothers in the UK, Rajan and Sanjay, had entered the family business of garment imports and had made their mark too after expanding it. They were both being featured in magazines whilst both my brothers in Delhi, Ajay and Sanjeev, had achieved celebrity status in the entertainment field. Family prestige and status meant the world to Indian families of my generation and I was careful not to damage it with a divorce. Not until I understood that my happiness could only uplift them and not bring them down in any way. However, when time was not on my side, the little that my parents knew about my predicament was not something they particularly wanted to entertain at that point, as divorce was a stigma in the '80s and most of the '90s. Most parents gently pushed their daughters back to their broken marriages to repair it with whatever it took! They took desperate measures to save their daughters marriages simply to save face from society. I had no magical superglue that could keep things from falling further apart. I was also told as a reassurance that no one's life is a fairy tale and the happily-ever-after is just a myth. What I did come to appreciate through the contrast of my life out there in England and life out here was the simplicity of my upbringing. I was suddenly nostalgic about my mother's aloo gobi, washing the dishes, table tennis, pool and my various other mundane activities besides gazing at the azure sky and writing poetry. In time, I was able to differentiate between good and bad, love and hate, arrogance and humility. I learnt through contrasts.

Only much later was I able to define my life with higher goals and ideals.

Despite familial and societal unwillingness, I abandoned my marriage twice only to go back to it resentfully and reluctantly. When time is not on your side, nothing moves. My life and my marriage, however, were certainly moving swiftly in the wrong direction.

4

The Difficult Road Ahead

There are two ways of meeting difficulties.
You alter the difficulties or you alter yourself to meet them.

Phyllis Bottome

In July 1997, my skin, already flared up with severe unsightly eczema, manifested something graver, more psychologically damaging and more physically debilitating. The situation had really got under my skin in a manner of speaking, and how!

A friend of mine suggested an astrologer she knew and although a part of me felt it would be pointless, there was a sense of urgency in me to know what lay ahead.

The short, semi-bald, stodgy and bespectacled astrologer—and the good Lord knows there are more of them on every street corner than a holy cow and a yellow three wheeler auto rickshaw in Delhi—carefully examined my birth chart, which he took endlessly long to peruse. He would slyly look at me, then revert to the chart many times over before he finally fixed his gaze on me from behind his densely cluttered desk. He was barely visible to me surrounded as he was by every Hindu deity's picture that I wasn't even aware existed! I thought my mother had introduced us to all of them but then clearly not, and every astrologer takes the support of one or the other or all of them to read into your future. It is as if all the trillion gods are chatting with the astrologer about your future whilst he reads your chart and then simply repeats what the gods have told him about you. I was half bored, a quarter curious and a quarter disgusted at myself for being there, and disgusted at him for pretending to know my future! To add to it, there were five or six incense sticks burning my lungs out along with a flame lit of clarified butter to illuminate a picture of Laxmi, the Goddess of Wealth. In the background he played bhajans at a volume so low that they could barely be heard. I think they were the 'Om' chant.

'Uh, Uh. What I say you? You look for a good doctor. No life after this year endz. You have a diss-easse? You very sick. Husbaand problem also? Children fine. No problem. Give me ₹15,000 and I pray for you, okay? 6 months and all will be well. Husband will be fine and you will live,' he reassured as he wobbled his semi-bald head, took off his spectacles and swung them vigorously in his right hand whilst he waited for a response from me. Then he joined his hands in reverence and bowed his head to all the gods that sat uncomfortably on his cluttered desk. 'Have faith in me! I will pray for you and you will be good,' he concluded with a smile that almost appeared sinister.

I sighed, letting out one deep breath and a forced smile before I abruptly rose from my seat, thanked him for his brief reading and without much ado I exited his office with a feeling of relief. I paid him his dues and no more. Despite his promise to move heaven and earth for me, I left without a single word. I sat in my car and my head began to talk as it customarily did:

'Hey Anita, your painful journey is almost over anyway so why crib anymore. Your in-laws will take care of your daughters. Go home and have your tea and chill with a good book, your truest companion in all these lonely years. All your anxieties will be laid to rest. Hurray!'

On reaching home, I went to the bathroom after switching off the light as had become customary, to avoid my hideous reflection. Laden with grief and anguish, I stood vulnerably in the dark bathroom to cry a well of tears. Not once did I negotiate with God. I had stopped doing that a long time ago. My conversations with him ended when my misery began. Writing letters to him as a child was limited to that phase of my life. I no longer penned my sentiments or expressed my love in poetry. In fact, the last time I had penned down any sentiments was when I had my first separation with my husband. I was in England and he, in India, and the expression was a desperate attempt for him to understand what I was going through, possibly to make him realise that we needed to bridge the growing gap with love. My collection of poems proved to be a futile attempt at reconciliation.

As I understood it then, he, God, either loved me excessively or not at all. I was just plain confused about him, very nearly not believing in Him and that translated into my prayer-less routine. The veil of ignorance had lifted with the passage of time, with my unending experiences, my unceasing trials and trepidations. My tête-à-têtes were no longer with God but with my own mind. It had been a figment of my very vivid imagination. My clever, chatty mind had concocted ceaseless heart-to-heart chats with him. I ceased to write a journal too that ended my day with 'Dear God...Thank you, God!' I believed that I had matured, possibly grown up and moved into a space of practicality as I had seen a reality more harsh than my innocent 12-year-old mind could have ever imagined. I began to believe that even if there was a God, he was for others and didn't have time to get round

25

to my issues. I needed the tide to turn before I drowned in the sea of despair.

In August 1997, my skin broke out like never before, with pus and an intolerable burning sensation. All I would do was place a cold towel on it and lie down. It would bleed and remain constantly red, inflamed, blotchy and unbearably itchy. I knew it wasn't eczema. It was far more serious but I still did not call out to God. God? Who God?

5

Sowing the Seed

The contrast between man's dream and his reality are
his inevitable awakening.

Anonymous

It was autumn of 1997, in the winter of my life. An acquaintance
then and a much-loved friend now called Bamby Singh visited
me at my home to persuade me to call upon her guru along
with her to seek his blessings. I resisted hard as I had met a
sufficient number of gurus, pundits and babas in Delhi since
my marriage. Every tenth person seemed like he had converted
himself into a spiritual guru for his livelihood. It was both
respectful and profitable and the need to consult one arises in
every Hindu man and woman's heart at some time or another to
either evade undesirable events or to invite the desirable ones.
Usually, the affluent pay pundits enormous amounts, leaving
them to negotiate with God to alter the course of their lives and

to break their bad karma. It's almost as if pundits have some deals going on with God. As if God even cares to entertain such absurdities of man. I didn't care much to involve myself with yet another guru. The astrologer I had visited was my attempt to gain a sense of where my life was heading and I never revisited him or any other after him. I was quite disconnected from the spiritual aspect of my life as nothing made good sense to me anymore and religion never piqued my curiosity either as I was definitely not a ritualistic or religious person. I was exasperated and exhausted.

Bamby initiated a dialogue with me that was almost convincing despite my resistance. 'Do you really have a choice? You are at the end of the road in any case, so even if you go bow before Him as a mark of respect, you have nothing to lose, do you?' She insisted trying hard not to look directly at me due to the severe inflammation on my face that made it appear almost deformed. My eyes were half shut with dried pus on the eyelids and there was dried blood on my chin from my excessive scratching. 'Your situation is insufferable and your skin is an indication of that. You will be a fool not to go.'

'How much will I need to carry with me as a donation or his fees? Is he expensive. Does he charge per session, or at the end of the so-called treatment?' I asked in a monotone without emotion or enthusiasm. Beyond a certain point, the body shuts down in a desperately stressful situation and you become mind blind. My series of questions were perfunctory and I tried hard to ask the right ones.

'I'm not going to even attempt to explain anything to you because His supremacy is beyond medical explanation and expenses, so kindly, do not belittle Him. He is incomprehensible to your tiny mortal mind but please do not reject Him without meeting Him,' she urged in a tone that was evidently irritable and defensive, yet controlled. 'Besides Anita, you think that you may not take to Him but it can be the other way too.'

'Oh okay,' I responded with a measure of cynicism and skepticism, and more than an ounce of inertia and indifference.

'He is God Himself, an avatar,' she insisted. 'He is the light of Shiva and has a trident in the creases of His forehead and an OM is shaped in his veins at the back of His bald head. He has come to uplift humanity from the self-destructive activities that they engage in and He can save you too from your illness.' Her large expressive eyes were filled with wonder and awe at the mention of his name but I almost didn't pay much heed to it. I just felt that this stunning looking woman was simply delusional! She had been swayed by the belief that a higher source guided her life and that source was within her reach in a physical form, in the shape of a guru. Maybe she had been brainwashed. Never mind, the philosopher in me thought, 'Live and let live.'

'I'll try him out I suppose,' I replied incoherently without the slightest bit of eagerness, expectation or anticipation. I was, however, eager to terminate this futile conversation. 'When do we go?' I asked almost without gratitude. I had stopped sugar-coating my words and often I would appear ungrateful and arrogant, particularly to those who didn't know me and Bamby certainly didn't at this point. I'm quite sure that her desire to take me to her guru was out of sheer empathy and humanity.

I let out an extended yawn as she fixed to meet on Thursday evening at 6 pm. Insomnia had taken over just to fan the flames, so I felt listless most of the time and I looked it all the time. In a word, I was plagued with negativity that sapped me of my energy. At this point in my journey, there was no oomph left in me.

'I'll fetch you and we'll go together to visit Shiva's avatar. Once you go to Him, your life will transform and you won't want to come back home. His divine abode will become your home. You are already blessed that you are going. It's your calling,' she reassured and offered a hug before adding, 'Trust me.'

I had heard this more times than I care to remember, particularly from people who had never looked the word 'trust' up in the dictionary. Hence, they understood it very loosely. What they meant was 'Trust me until I betray you!' 'Trust me because you're a fool!' 'Trust me because you love being cheated!'

'Thanks! I'll see you then. Thursday? 6?' I repeated with an obligatory smile and a cold hug. My eyes were expressionless. I waved her goodbye with a vacant look that too had almost become an integral part of my physical make-up. She squeezed my hand as if to reassure me that I was about to do the right thing. Her lips and eyes both smiled in unison and then she left after confirming the time and date.

A few minutes after she left, I lay down as I was jaded. My energy level was so low that I would wake up in the late hours of the morning, sleep after lunch, rise just before dusk and sleep again at night. I had exhausted my sleeping regime and even during my few waking hours, I would be in a slumber! The get-up-and-go in me had got-up-and-gone!

A few months earlier, Bamby had a conversation with me regarding her guru. Her brother, Pinto, his wife, Saira, my former husband and I had gone to watch *The Titanic*, the movie at PVR cinemas. Over there, just before the sinking of the 'Titanic', my heart started sinking and my asthma attack came on with a vengeance. They all observed my frantic wheezing and rushed me to my nursing home where I was customarily admitted during an attack— The Aashlok. I was under the gentle guidance of Dr Ashwani and Dr Alok Chopra who would administer steroid injections in the ICU and prescribe me steroid tablets subsequent to my discharge. They had both seen me at my worst and years later, they would see me at my best and even be startled at my still being around!

Bamby's brother, Pinto, had understood the gravity and the seriousness of my sickness as he had witnessed my attack. I lay in the ICU, careworn and sullen, appearing 20 years older than my actual years. I felt too old and too sick to want to recover. I was 32 years young, far from old. Yet, I lacked the zest and the zeal to ride out the storm.

Not only does sound health contribute to human happiness but a large measure of love is as imperative to bring us back from the grave. We all need a reason to go on and although I had my girls to think of, my mind was too disturbed and my body far too distressed. I needed a reason and that reason could've only been love.

I pulled through, though very grudgingly, arriving home after a few days of rest and respite in the nursing home before returning to the dreariness again. I was prescribed steroid tablets for several more weeks before being weaned off them. By this time I was largely overweight, hugely under-confident and hardly concerned about stepping up to my life. I was filled with sluggishness and indifference that became an integral part of my recent years. I was a walking zombie and maybe sleepwalking through the rest of my life would be easier as I wouldn't have to apply my mind to comprehend the root of my anguish and why the human spirit relinquishes its every desire in the face of hopelessness. I had even renounced my longing to seek solace and support. In brief, I was languid and was just killing time before it killed me as the astrologer had predicted, especially since I hadn't paid him to extend my life!

I loved him since I was a child, wrote to him, spoke to him in the open skies, even urged him to have tea with me, and what did he do to reciprocate? He simply threw me into a muddy pond and commanded me to sink or swim. I was sinking and at this point I realised that it was God who was an illusion, not my mother cooking aloo gobi and my father driving up the driveway in his Rolls Royce. The laughter of the children next door and the cars driving by were all real-life experiences. I heard the table-tennis ball of my childhood echo in my head. I even reminisced about the mundane school routine and its strictness where my tie had to be tied till the top button of my white shirt, something that almost throttled me! My blue uniform of a short skirt, white shirt, yellow tie and blazer in a conservative private school for all girls suddenly became a delightful memory. At the time, I didn't think much of the stringent atmosphere of my school or its education. The real education is outside the classroom and I will still not glorify past experiences particularly school days to state that they were the best days of my life as people customarily state because each time I was told that, I remember thinking in my head, 'Are you serious? You mean life doesn't get any better!'

My sickness too, was as real and as tangible as could possibly be. My heartache and loneliness too could be held in both the hands and their weight quantified. Everything had substance and mass. Every emotion could be measured and defined.

Our distress is as real as are our dreams. Our every thought carries energy and it is that energy that is transmitted to every cell, tissue and fibre of our anatomy and every molecule of our being. Hence, it is imperative to entertain 'happy thoughts', to have 'happy cells.' The cells in our body need a healthy and robust atmosphere to regenerate just as our mind needs a happy and peaceful environment to encourage positive thoughts that directly impact the body. If the environment that we dwell in is not conducive to either our health or happiness, then the situation needs to be evaluated. The space we dwell in determines our personal and spiritual growth. It can either make us or break us.

Human life is far from an illusion. Our every struggle, strife and suffocation is real and no one's is greater or smaller since the sufferer knows its depth and the influence it has on our body, mind and spirit. The solutions others may have for us may not necessary be the ones that may work for us, as they are so individual and unique. No one really knows us, but knows only his/her perception of us. However, our lives are open to interpretation and judgment by others. Those too are real.

How real was the umpteenth guru I was to meet on Thursday would shortly be revealed but how real was my faith I already knew. Zilch faith, zero fascination and zip feelings. I had faith in my situation getting progressively worse. The number of mere mortals converting themselves into long, grey-bearded gurus fascinated me and I had real feelings of pain and anguish.

The beginning was perfunctory and obligatory as Bamby was not only an acquaintance who meant well but she was also my former husband's client who had very recently purchased a car from him. In addition, I was at the end of the road in any case, so what the heck!

I sat in her plush car and we drove off to the so-called divine domain. I didn't pay any heed to the road that led us to our destination neither did I calculate the length of time it was taking us. I was oblivious to the journey, the environs that we passed and my thoughts. I sat in utter silence, not because I was reflective or meditative but because I really had nothing to say. I said nothing for it probably meant close to nothing. It was that simple.

It was NOT simple at all!

6

A Date with God

Truth is stranger than fiction.

Mark Twain

We finally arrived at an inexplicable and extraordinary situation
that did not give me the liberty of lending it expression. It was
inscrutable and enigmatic. Even with my articulation, I could not
characterise and describe this moment. It was nothing I had ever
experienced. I was dumbstruck, stupefied, amused, bemused and
hopelessly confused! I lost my power of speech but all my other
senses came alive. I couldn't think or blink and because I was so
overwhelmed, the lump in my throat just got bigger with each
passing moment. Now I was more dazed than ever! I didn't know
whether to hoot or to stay mute!

No long flowing salt-and-pepper beard. No plain saffron
cotton robe and no rosemary beads heavily wrapped around
His neck or between His thumb and index finger and no red or

orange colour smeared in the centre of His forehead. To top it all, no donation bowl was sitting next to Him in keen anticipation!

Instead, what I observed was a man with the most resplendent clean-shaven head, radiant face that glowed like a heavenly lamp against the dim backdrop of the earthly human struggle. He wore a majestically tailored, saffron silken garb that was splendidly embroidered and long enough to cover His feet. A dazzling gold and diamond-studded watch adorned his wrist. His skin was enviably radiant, almost translucent and His compassion-filled eyes were transfixed on me as I steadily walked towards Him to bow my head to His feet that were in bejewelled jootis (shoes). He wore His stillness and His silence even amid my life's noise. In a word, as no amount of words can accurately measure the depth of my feeling at that moment, He had the most distinct personality that I had yet to come across and an aura that filled me with an overwhelming longing to know more. According to a Buddhist proverb, 'When the student is, ready the teacher appears.'

The room was practically empty with fresh flowers sitting on the sideboard adjacent to the kitchen and there was a music system placed on the far end of the room. The floor was carpeted and scrupulously clean and there was a luminosity that permeated the room. An energy I was unfamiliar with drew me in, filling me with a drive to know more. He sat on a golden throne-like chair but then it was a throne as He reigned in His disciples' hearts. My own lightened heart was full of marvel and awe. He smiled. I smiled. Bamby laughed!

I sat humbly on the floor as you are expected to but instead of my head bowing down, I blatantly looked up at Him looking at me! He was beautiful and I fell in love with Him! I felt elated and ecstatic to say the least and my experience was not at all in line with my expectations. I had been a lost child whose mother had found her but then He was the personification of more than that. He was everything my soul was searching for and expressing gratitude in my head, I heaved a deep sigh of relief and release.

He said nothing, Bamby said little and I said it all in my mind except I had an uncontainable urge to vocally spill it all out until the entire place was flooded with my tears, fears and every other heaving emotion that I had carried over the years. By this time, I was nine years into my marriage and I had plenty to say!

Hug me tight, locking me in your eternal clasp. Rejuvenate me, redeem me, rescue me, reincarnate me, revive me, and restore my spirit to reawaken me to my truth, your truth, the universal truth. Please do all of this and much more. Simply breathe new life into me as I know You will and don't send me back to that hellhole that is supposed to be my home. I know I made a pledge to love him till death do us part but I cannot live with him any longer. For that I beg for forgiveness but I have many valid reasons. Keep me here instead and I'll sweep Your floor, clean the loo, wash the clothes, cook and wash all the dishes a thousand times over but promise not to send me back home. I implored in my mind. My head sure could talk! I was tongue-tied but my eyes spoke volumes, as did my never-ending, chattering mind!

He, Guruji, heard my telepathic plea and felt my desperate appeal as He smiled at me reassuringly whilst He was still scanning me. He knew. I knew He knew and Bamby most definitely knew! The soul language is spoken not with words but with vibrations shared between people on the same frequency. Bamby and I had become one in this moment and Guruji who was beyond anything the human mind can imagine, observed this phenomenon. In that one inexplicable moment, my search was over.

Before I averted my shamelessly fixed gaze from Him, I picked up the whiff of a fragrance comparable to a larger than life-sized bouquet of roses. I took my gaze away from Him momentarily to catch that bouquet. Nope! It was nowhere to be seen. Perhaps there is a rose garden outside, I reasoned. Maybe He sprays a rose perfume all over Himself very liberally indeed. What, the entire bottle? Yes and so what? I inhaled the aroma deep into my lungs like some magic potion that was going to dissolve all my hurt and disband my karmic bondage. I was perked up momentarily as I let go and let God take over. I silently acknowledged my teenage wisdom of knowing that something extraordinary awaited me and I hadn't, after all, lived in a paradise of illusions.

My initial encounter with Him was very nearly silent and my mind too became quiet after the preliminary mental dialogue! The relentless chat of my over-analytical mind was hushed momentarily, which was indeed a miracle, the first of many although I was becoming increasingly desperate to explode before Him. The reservoir of questions and the well of emotions that choked my throat wanted to overflow. Instead, I sat in dignified silence. The boisterous voice inside of me told me that He is Master know-all-and-be-all, so stay mum. Be wise rather than otherwise, or my chance of any divine intervention will be lost. I didn't wish to belittle His greatness by either asking or by telling Him anything although later on, I did speak on many occasions out of the sheer desperation of no longer being able to hold my tongue. I conversed with Him as I would with my father, mother, brother, friend or councillor but at that moment, I was writing a gratitude letter to the heavens in my mind. 'Thank you all the angels, fairies, spiritual guides, Celestial this and that and God Himself! You are all too kind! Take care and have a good day!' I must have done something right in my life or in my past lives to have earned this moment. In this extraordinarily exclusive moment, I was grateful for all the wrong I had done, the karmic suffering and the subsequent road that it had lead me to. Without darkness, I would not have sought light.

My eyes, very cautiously scanned the room to see what or who else could be viewed. There were large animated photos of Him adorning every wall in the room. In the heart of the room hung an electric blue chandelier resembling the striking Italian Murano crystal, that emitted a radiance I was not acquainted with before.

And then I noticed His penetrating eyes were still scanning me! It was as though He were reading chapter and verse on all my previous lives as well as this one and possibly the one after this! He looked straight into my soul or so it seemed. He knew the mistakes I had made and the ones He needed to erase. He may have wondered where to begin with a project that had no end! Subsequently, He still sat calmly with absolute compassion and willingness to alter my destiny without judgment. *I am profoundly sorry for all the wrong that I have done knowingly or unknowingly.* He did not utter much and I spoke little as I found His native Punjabi language close to Latin! I understood less of the very little something He uttered but I was at ease in His presence almost immediately on sitting before Him. Bamby very skillfully translated His expressions in English and Hindi. I was oblivious to how much time had elapsed in scrutinising one another and getting a sense of what was happening. I was so contented that I longed for time to freeze. I also felt butterflies flutter violently in my stomach for fear of Him taking the skeletons out of the closet! I somehow knew that He knew it all. He was absolute and that is the reason I felt complete at the first instance. It was faith and love at first sight. Bamby's 'Trust me' had more substance than I had ever known before and my belief in trust had been restored instantly as had my vision of something great that I had imagined as a teenager. The asthma, eczema, the hole in the heart, the endless hospital stays along with my ailing marriage, all had a deeper purpose. In the midst of difficulty lies opportunity.

As I sat wondering what He would reveal after examining me, I experienced yet another aroma, an aroma all too familiar to me and to my senses. I should have jumped out of my skin but it was His grace and presence that kept me centred and calm even amidst my inner turmoil that was about to dissolve forever.

He quietly gestured the disciple who worked selflessly in the kitchen to place the piping hot glass of tea before me. I stared at the tea aghast as if it were an old friend that just popped its head into my life at the most unexpected hour after many years of disappearance. I glanced up at Him and He smiled knowingly.

No, He was not an old friend but a timeless one who was about to become my eternal Guide, Guard and God.

I released lifetimes of tears in my heart, tears of bliss, tears of a divine kiss and tears of sorrow untold.

'So here You are. You drove me through the darkest of dark to transport me to light, Your light. This may have been Your celestial strategy but how could I possibly grow in the shadows. I sit here before You, shrivelled and shrunk. What else could You expect other than a heavy and forlorn heart? I proclaimed my most innocent and childlike love for You more times than I could commit to memory but I clearly recall the particular day when my mother was cooking her trillionth aloo gobi and You were painting the sky with impeccable strokes of azure blue hues on a cloudless day. Such perfection is a rare view on England's canvas and its exuberance is imprinted on my mind's landscape. A child of that age generally doesn't express her love for God with such passion as it is usually engaged in more childlike activities but I was different, perhaps owing to my congenital illnesses I began to see things differently. I transcended the teenage vanities and other trivialities as I felt life had to have much more to offer me for me to give it meaning and purpose.

You, however, reciprocated my affection and adoration by casting me into a deep dark hole, expecting me to climb out of it. Come on Guruji, give me a break! Despite my worst accumulated karmas of countless lifetimes of which I have no recollection, I insist that I didn't earn this lot but You imposed it on me for perhaps a more noble cause! The unending chain of cause and effect is obscure to my mind but I am sure You will lend me clarity with the passage of time. Perhaps You were testing me, polishing me, making me worthy of Your love? Whatever it was, it has marred and miffed my spirit. It has offended me terribly but I'm not here to cry my woes to You or to pay my dues. I am here for clarity as only You can grasp the degree of my suffering. You do, don't You? Maybe You do feel that I earned my lot, a kind of karmic retribution. What goes around comes around, so I deserve every bit of what I get. Well, for now, I'm reasonably clear that I'm here to soak in this long-awaited moment with You and I commit to You with depth of devotion. This experience is as surreal as it is real. Now that I have found You, I am ready to lose myself in You.'

The heaviness in my heart was lightened, as I was in no doubt that this Guru was not here to make a grand fool out of me. He was here to take the fool out of me, to renovate the dark, ignorant room of my mind and to refurbish the stripped-down walls of my heart. Light and dark exist within each one of us. He was here to teach us how to dispel our dark with our inherent light.

I carefully picked up the warm glass and felt it, my hands gently shaking with nervous energy. I embraced it, clasped my hands around the glass while I gazed up at Him engagingly. Then, with that knowing smile, He commanded gently and graciously, 'Drink it, this is your blessing.'

'It sure is mate!' I gladly thought to myself with my mind driven by the nostalgia of my British slang!

I sipped the divine tea ponderingly and purposely with the oversized lump stuck bravely in my throat. I was almost reduced to tears but I did not bawl! Instead, my lungs exhaled an extended, exuberant breath that silently said, 'I will survive!' I had, after lifetimes of drifting, arrived home. What the soul seeks the soul finds. And truly, 'If it never rained, nothing would ever grow.'

7

The Healing

Life is not about waiting for the storm to pass.
It is about learning to dance in the rain.

Anonymous

The feeling of elation is very often accompanied with the feeling
of desolation. As I sat comfortably before Guruji, the embodiment
of the divine, my heart was full of relief at having found Him, yet
disbelief at it being too good to be true. Maybe this is a tease and
in a flash it will all be taken away from me. The fear of losing
remains constant. 'Love me little, love me long.'

This innate fear of losing resides within each one of us and
very often drives us away from knowing the joy that exists in
the moment since angst takes over ruthlessly. Each time I sat
with Guruji, the feeling of losing Him would make me lose the
pleasure of His presence. He knew only too well that my mind was

everywhere except with Him and He would gently manoeuvre me back by reassuring me that the mentor-disciple relationship is a symbiotic one. If I need Him, then He needs me too for His worship. It is an eternal bond that begins in the here and now, so to remain present is essential to one's spiritual growth. Being in the moment significantly suffuses your spirit with the divine spirit to make it one. He would often nudge me to pay more attention to the devotional songs that were playing and to the experiences that other devotees shared about their life-changing blessings that Guruji had bestowed on them.

'Tune yourself to the shabad (divine songs) and the chai prasad (blessed tea,) relish the langar (blessed food) and listen attentively to other people's experiences. These are collectively breaking many lifetimes of your karma as well as clearing your path for your future,' He summoned. 'Have you known anything to be easier in redeeming yourself? You may not know it yet but you are blessed just to be here. How far you go is up to you, so be wise. Your free will plays a pivotal role in the amount of blessings you accumulate. You can go the wrong way or choose to be on the path to salvation. This precious time cannot be recaptured, so don't lose it in needless worry and fear.'

He would say little and I would understand even less. I suppose words couldn't lend expression to my experiences with Him in any case, so less was more in a way. Besides, His Punjabi accent was almost incomprehensible but I completely understood the reason for my being there and that was sufficient. Blessed me had been given this extraordinary opportunity to sit beside Him every day amongst thousands of other disciples who had taken a leap of faith by turning up at His divine abode day after day. New faces would be seen every day along with some familiar ones from my social circle and others from eminent circles. Celebrities would park themselves comfortably before Him and Guruji always made it a point to introduce me to all of them. In hindsight, He was breathing new life into my isolated existence. Fortunately for me, my daughters, Anishka and Sonakshi, also started accompanying me on some days for langar. They were 5 and 6 years old at the time and looking back, I'm grateful for the blessings that Guruji showered on them. They used to fall asleep whilst sitting there but on the arrival of the langar, they would wake up with a jolt and relish every bite! After taking a step back, I also realise the protection He had given them for the impending trying and tiresome times.

What I observed in His mounting following was a new face every day and yet the gatherings were so manageable and controlled. What was uncontrollable, though, was the electric energy that flowed through His disciples whilst they sat in His presence. Some cried whilst others smiled with a joy that you feel when an unexpected happiness comes your way, a kind of surprise. Surrendering to Him meant opening yourself up to many surprises that come to light at every corner of your life at the most unexpected moments. It was all for a good reason. Only He knew what each soul needs. We only know what we want and there is always a fine line between the two.

Truth has its own gravity and its force pulls people towards it naturally and effortlessly. Guruji was the magnet and whether or not people realised the tangible differences in their lives, they knew instinctively that there were some internal benefits they felt that went far beyond the tangible and the material. His following grew by leaps and bounds on a minute-to-minute basis. Watching people flood in gave me a wave of personal joy as if by them being blessed, I too would benefit! Witnessing optimism on people's faces inexplicably renders us hope and a shared joy. Their beaming faces are contagious almost validating the goodness of the object of your worship. It is also commendable how they are well entrenched in their faith, be it rain or shine in their lives. I, the grand cynic, needed to light a torch to see if the sun really is there and I do believe there are many who fall in my category. Faith has a heart but no mind.

I parked myself every evening in the same cozy space on the floor where I could gaze up at Him and sip my tea whilst soaking in His devotional songs and His all-pervading aura. I had truly found my shelter in His durbar (divine audience). At just past 9 pm, the langar would be served and He placed great emphasis on consuming it, as if it were medicine to cure all ailments, from physical to emotional, financial as well as spiritual. Every individual came with one or the other or more but the issues were practically the same as we are all part of the collective destiny of a shared humanity. I knew I needed healing on more levels than one, so I ate ravenously and always hoped to be served more! With a resounding yes, I obeyed His every command. In time, I began to witness other devotees being healed with the power of the langar that cured the gentlest ailments to the most ghastly ones. From time to time, He would give me a supportive smile that would provide me the strength to weather my ordeals too.

Healing was a process that did not happen overnight but His presence was enough to reassure me that all will be well, so hang in there woman! On days when my daughters accompanied me as instructed by Him then, His focus shifted to them. He told me that they are very bright and beautiful girls in and out. I knew then that He was shielding them and giving them a sense of security and safety.

After a few visits, He suggested I remove my gem studded rings that I wore on virtually every finger to evade something or another! The superstition was instilled in me by one of my countless pundits! Guruji let out a roaring laughter as He asked me gently how much the notorious pundit made out of me for prescribing the various semi-precious stones. I replied sheepishly as I realised how much I had been conned. Desperate situations require desperate measures. One of them even suggested that I place a large gemstone in my former husband's wardrobe to dilute his anger and to make him love me! Yeah, right! If only stones could do the trick of melting hearts, I would have kept one in George Clooney's wardrobe for sure. My only plight then would be how to get there in the first place. Perhaps I would pay yet another pundit to give me a route map to his residence and then to his wardrobe that would then give me access to his other more inviting pieces of furniture!

I do believe that on meeting Guruji, my desire to seek guidance from other myriad psychics, sages, seers, avatars, new-age pundits and wanna-be gurus, idols, councillors and past-life regression therapists as well as hypnotists, diluted in a hurry though my appetite for diverse spiritual and mystical experiences was and would remain insatiable. My most engaging experiences were with my Guruji and those would remain unparalleled by any other. The divine romance and dance between a mentor and disciple can only be learnt through experiential knowledge, not through intellectual learning. It is through the extraordinary act of fate that I was able to experience this phenomenon. I could engage myself in more theories than one but the only way to really change my karma and for Him to re-write my destiny was for me to surrender. To accept and not to expect was the order of the day but then a mere mortal like me did very little to live by this motto.

It was early September in 1997 when I made that very first entry to my haven and thereafter, I took His word as law when He instructed me to visit Him every day for healing. Come rain or shine, I would be at His darbar every evening by 6.30 pm or so. After the changing season in October, I was convinced that He had performed His first miracle of curing my asthma: I had not had my inevitable attack for the first time since I'd been residing in Delhi. It will only be right to say though that the skeptic in me dismissed it as sheer coincidence! I recall getting the asthma attack whilst sitting in His presence and Guruji and I got into a tussle as I insisted on leaving whilst He insisted on me not only staying but also consuming the langar. I was angry and agitated as I felt that He was being insensitive to my situation as all I really needed was hospitalisation as had become customary

45

in all my years. I needed steroids and He insisted that the food was both my steroids and oxygen! He told me very sternly that if I was to get healed, then I needed to make sure that I ate every morsel of the food! Of course I was reduced to tears and I ate forcefully and as I touched His feet to leave, I telepathically said, 'I will not come here ever again as You are insensitive!' Right away He responded, 'Come tomorrow and now go home and sleep peacefully! I have healed you. You are blessed!'

It was not until seasons came and went over the subsequent years that I realised the absence of the attacks as well as the long awaited absence of predisolone, the cortisone tablets that I had been taking for years, from anything between 5 mg to 30 mg, that had already left behind many side effects. One of them was the development of cataract in both my eyes at the age of 31. Dr Pakrasi, a highly proficient surgeon performed my surgery at Aashlok Hospital soon after it was detected. He subsequently became a good friend, as I couldn't thank him enough for restoring my vision.

My spiritual vision was also becoming clearer and I came to my senses only to realise that Guruji is Divinity, Shiva incarnate and, hopefully, we were united in the clasp of eternity unless I slipped and wandered off by the wayside. I believe that there had already been an endlessly long absence from myself and now was the time to be introduced to my true self through Guruji. The rough journey of the soul was nearing its end and a new dawn was around the corner. Of that I was sure.

After several months of a spiritual awakening, I began to converse with Him in an easy, casual and comfortable manner and we would often break into humour about my British accent and His native Punjabi one! I also learnt that His English was impeccable when one fine day He broke into it when I had shamefully asked Him to repeat Himself on not understanding Him. After a certain point, the language of love was all that was required to bridge the linguistic gap and I reached a place where I no longer needed to lend expression to my thoughts. I would sit in companionable silence whilst maintaining a spiritual connection with Him. Sometimes the silence between us said it all. As time went by and the changes within me became apparent, many of my doubts about Him were ironed out but of course never totally. The nature of doubt is to return whenever a cloud descends.

The conducive environment of the temple charged my body and soul with the current of spirituality. India, without a shadow of doubt, is the right setting for spiritual growth as it has been blessed with a rich history of avatars who descended to the abode of man to uplift him and show him his true image. It is through sacred teachings as applicable today as they were then, along with meditation techniques that draw people from various cultures around the world to India to various sites. I personally visited Rishikesh once on a blindingly sunny and hot day only to realise that the austere routine of meditators rising at 4 am and making their connection with the divine practically all day with very little consumption of food was not for me! I was inspired to visit it by virtue of John Lennon's love for it and the many recordings he made during his stay there. In fact, the Beatles stayed at the Maharishi's ashram for lengthy periods of time. As for me, I became ever more grateful for Guruji's undemanding and uncomplicated philosophy that allowed me to consume His energy as well as the food in abundance and still hope to attain moksha (liberation). Instead of dipping into the holy river, I immersed myself totally in Guruji's light. Somewhere in my subconscious, I too wanted to learn about myself and I was probably precisely where I had longed to be—as a child. Thankfully I didn't need to endure long hours of silence and starvation here at Guruji's! His teachings were practical and applicable to everyday life without having to give up anything, especially one's comforts. I was in an unfathomable bliss despite my physical and emotional torment. The satisfaction of being in His divine presence a few hours each day, overrode the unhappiness in my life. Soon I realised that I was married to my faith and I prayed never to be divorced from it. I wanted to grow from it, then branch out to touch others lives that were also in dire need. Only Guruji could tighten the knot.

Meanwhile, my skin was causing increasing physiological and psychological pain. Yet, the only blessing I considered appropriate at that point was for Him to grant me the big D. Patience was never one of my greatest virtues, especially now that I had found my magician with the magic wand who could grant me all my wishes, or perhaps not. We ask for that which we want and He gives us that which we need.

'Guruji?' I began under my nose on an evening when I sat beside Him, feeling emotionally very drained. I was so overwhelmed that I was almost beside myself and I dared to ask but was silenced before I could.

'Don't ask for that which I cannot grant you,' He insisted. 'Humans need to see the deeper meaning in suffering and also to understand its ephemeral nature. This too shall pass and with time; things will change. Be patient.' He continued, 'Your life may be falling apart but if you have absolute faith in me, then things will fall into place. Just keep coming. That is all you need to do. Learn to accept and not expect.'

I frowned. He smiled. I closed my eyes to resign to my situation and cry silently for only my soul to hear my scream. 'Is there anyone out there who understands what I'm going through because it seems like even He doesn't? Perhaps He too blames me.' My growing sense of frustration was gnawing at my peace of mind, of which I had very little left. Life's lessons don't come as gently as the tickle of a feather. They are often long and hard and test us ruthlessly to shake our core.

Two seasons had come and gone and my asthma hadn't been triggered. I knew without question that my respiratory condition had been taken care of by my Guruji. He had embraced me like no other and yet I resented Him for holding me captive in my marriage. The truth is that when we are not granted what we believe is rightfully ours, we hold a secret resentment towards He who has the power to bring about the change we want or need. We tend to marginalise the journey of the soul as our focus is primarily the physical body and its needs. In that sense, what I realised was that I had not really surrendered to Him, as I did not entirely trust His judgment of my situation and the imperativeness of my divorce.

My faith, of course, swayed like a pendulum and would move up and down, so if I were on step 8 at one given point, I would suddenly descend to step 2 if I felt disappointed by Him. I would even go to the extent of doubting His supremacy. My thoughts would be reduced to, 'Guruji is an ordinary Guru with extraordinary powers.' My pea-sized brain was convinced that life had rewarded Him for His past-life good karmas and now He was here to heal us but He was incapable of granting me the big D. In my limited vision, I believed that even His ability to bless me was limited and my demanding a divorce was a definite 'no-go area.' Healing me of my asthma was suddenly not viewed by me as an unmixed blessing. I watered down His supremacy owing to my own personal grievances that clouded my judgment of Him.

The paradox, however, was that during the years that He kept denying me the big D, He would tell me not to introduce myself to others as Anita Bagla. He would say, 'Just say Anita!' Then in 2004, He advised me to approach my father to make me secure financially, which completely confused me. To this, I emphatically responded, 'Guruji, I am married and in Punjabi families of my generation, fathers pass everything on to their sons, so where do I figure in and for what purpose would he need to make me secure? I'm married and my husband needs to do that.'

I was baffled as in one breath He would deny me turning my back on my marriage and then in the next breath he would insist that my father save my back! He instructed me several times to speak to my father before I finally flew to England to shyly ask him to make me secure to which his response was surprisingly in the affirmative. I made no bones about telling my father that this was Guruji's hukum (divine order). I told him that by making me secure, Guruji was blessing him.

By this time, my father had been struck with cancer for the umpteenth time and he was undergoing chemotherapy. On this brief trip of mine, my father had done the needful and on returning to Guruji, He asked, 'Has your father made you secure then? Now you are financially fine?' I understood little as I found this whole practice contradictory to His hukum. However, I continued my journey with Guruji and in all my getting, I was forgetting that He was road-mapping my life. When we cannot see, we blindingly accuse, blame and criticise (ABC). The ABC attitude of mine towards Guruji belittled my own integrity in faith that was so absurdly selfish, based on, 'which of my wishes has He granted to which ones He hasn't.' It had become all about ticking the boxes as if He were my genie. Such was my ridiculously small mind, and smaller heart that was always eager to receive from Him but never ready to give Him in terms of unconditional love and devotion. A devotee's love, by and large, is conditional whilst His is purely unconditional.

He gazed at me with His eyes full of compassion and asked, 'Do you know what "Guru" means?'

'No,' I responded plainly.

'The guru removes the darkness (gu) of ignorance with the light (ru) of wisdom. In this nation's sacred tradition, the guru is put on a pedestal even higher than that of God. He is seen as the sine qua non of the spiritual journey. My dear Anita, enjoy the journey by surrendering to it positively,' ordered Guruji tenderly. 'I can see that which you cannot. Hence, believe that all that you receive is what is good for you and that which has not yet come to you is also to your benefit. You can see till this wall whereas my vision is infinite as I see way beyond.'

Most of my contentions were merely telepathic as I lacked the courage to ask for anything other than sound health, the greatest wealth but then I felt truly impoverished even by that when there was no real happiness in my home. I recall one such incident when after a turbulent encounter at home, I had rushed to His divine abode to plead with Him to disentangle the threads of my karma. 'What's the big deal? You bless many others for a break up and their grievances are probably not half as grave as mine. Yet, You choose not to liberate me from this unspeakable pain. What do I say or do to convince You that I have no marriage?' I burst out. I could no longer contain myself as my emotions spilled over hysterically. 'Either change him or change my destiny,' I pleaded desperately and this time my dialogues with Him were not telepathic. I had never been as vocal as I had been that evening. He looked at me as He usually did, most affectionately, but this time with deep concern. For the very first time, I observed Guruji's expression change from serene to sad. He turned pensive as he listened to my unspeakable pain. I spoke audibly and audaciously.

I cried before Him with tears rolling down my cheeks ceaselessly. I bared my soul to Him without dressing it up with fine words. My truth poured out as callously as was my situation and I was not remotely aware of the many eyes resting on me while I sobbed restlessly and relentlessly. My angst had clearly overwhelmed me to the point where I could no longer contain it and it spilled all over Guruji. I didn't edit my words neither did I swallow my grievances. I did not ask either. Instead I commanded. I pleaded. I cried and that too inconsolably as though the reservoir of tears stored within me were anxiously waiting to be released. The mellifluous devotional songs played in the background to unlock the hidden truths within us that Guruji insisted we meditate on during the hour or two of being in that sacred space. I did not even listen. Chai prasad was served lavishly and lovingly by the subservient disciples. I did not drink. The aromatic langar was served to the desiring disciples longing to be healed at every human level. I refused to eat.

Guruji and I were frozen in that moment. His penetrating eyes revealed sadness, remorse and compassion, all rolled into one. He felt sadness for the karma I had unknowingly created, remorse for not being able to break the karma of a disciple whom He truly loved and compassion towards the person who inflicted my anguish.

I had yet to see Him so engrossed in His thoughts and so unbelievably pensive. Through my tears I looked up at Him and without embellishing my words I urged, 'Guruji, I refuse to live with him. Please, I refuse to live with him.'

I was imprisoned in my situation; I was captive of my karma. I was locked up in a cell of despair to which only Guruji had the key. I had surrendered my most hopeless issue to Him. His gaze did not abandon me. He watched me as I spoke intermittently through my blinding tears. I had never wept as profusely and as profoundly as I did that evening. I was oblivious to my sacred surroundings. I was wrapped up in many layers of my own dejection and dismay. 'Please help me, please help me' was my silent as well as vocal plea.

He did not smile as he usually did. Instead, He frowned and He was still pensive and preoccupied. He continued to sit on His gaddi (divine seat). Disciples came and went after bowing to Him in reverence. His gaze was transfixed. He refused to utter a word. I refused to leave His side. I sat obstinately, crying openly. I needed Him to hear me, to audibly hear the unspeakable cries of my heart, soul and every other facet of my being.

Any normal, self-respecting person would not have let their guard down with such audacity before hundreds of others and though they could not entirely hear us, our expressions spoke volumes for others to get an idea of the situation. My melancholy was far greater than my desire to save face. I sat before Him and before others entirely vulnerable. 'I am miserable and for that I am sorry but I AM miserable. I can dress misery in a pretty, luscious fabric and dye it in attractive hues but its very essence will still be MISERY. I have taken off my garb of pretence to bare my misery to you. I have been left with no choice. My heart hurts, my spirit hurts and God knows my skin is breaking out every milli-second and that too hurts. I am certain that besides every tissue, fibre, cell, muscle and bone in my body, all the astral and heavenly bodies are also hurting for me. The ant on the floor walking towards me is also hurting for me and so is the lizard on the wall behind You, which I usually abhor but am somehow indifferent to tonight.

'And above all, my caring compassionate Guruji, I also know for sure that You too are hurting for me. So what's the score? Are we going to sit here in the height of misery till the length and breadth of eternity?

'My unhappiness cannot be measured but I do know that if You so desire, You do have the ability to rule it out completely. Only You can, inch by inch, remove my bad karma or else why would You be considered the Supreme Being, the All-knowing, the All-pervading and the Omnipresent. Although at this point, only my despair seems to be omnipresent and my sadness all-pervading.'

My tears stopped. I had no sense of time, so I'm unable to recollect for how long I had been crying my woes but I did feel tons lighter. My well had emptied and I felt unburdened from years of woe. It was almost cathartic. He seemed like He suddenly came out of a trance as He motioned all to leave and return to their respective homes. He motioned one of the disciples to serve me tea as I sat still at His feet. I sipped it slowly as I always did, hoping that my glass would remain full!

I was exhausted and energised in the same breath as I was both tranquil and turbulent too. He then ordered one of the disciples to prepare fresh halwa (blessed sweet) while I composed myself and prepared to leave after consuming it. I soon realised that I was famished! Every bite melted in my mouth as I savoured its flavour and aroma as it replenished and revitalised me. I gazed up at Him satisfied and nourished to the core. The magic of food! After a few minutes, He very gently ordered me to return home and to revisit Him the following evening. I left calmly as I was no longer afraid. My loss of faith over the years had disorientated me but now my vacuum was filled with His deep empathy and love. He was teaching me the lesson of love that began with the self. I knew that life would not be the same after this night was over.

The truth, as proclaimed by artists, poets and philosophers, is that love is the ultimate goal of man. Love can also be experienced through simple loving contemplation of the image an individual carries of a beloved. Love goes beyond the physical person, so the mental imagery and conversation can be as vivid and fulfilling. The longing for one's presence ceases, as one is already present. These sentiments summed up my relationship with my Guruji.

'Love many things, for therein lies true strength, and whosoever loves much performs much, and can accomplish much, and what is done in love is done well,' Vincent Van Gogh had said.

The daily visits had become the light at the end of my dismal tunnel as, besides His blessings, they allowed me to interact with the still small voice of calm within that revealed my truth. I was nowhere close to meeting God in the temple of my body as I couldn't sit still after two or more restless minutes in meditation, so I met Him outside myself instead, that too with absolute, unwavering faith and pure love. I no longer felt lonely or fearful after that night. I knew I would change radically and my world would not be the same again. As He had summoned many times: 'Contemplate my name and image and you will find me beside you. Live with courage and not fear. God is courage and the demon is fear.'

I was filled with so much peace now that I believed I could disengage my mind from my domestic surroundings. The inner equanimity is not moved by the turbulent climate on the outside. After bowing, I gazed penetratingly into His compassionate and knowing eyes. He looked directly into mine and at that moment,I knew that faith had to be all or nothing and something urged me to 'surrender.' He knew me up close and personal, so He also knew the formula for my happiness but was I ready to surrender? And what did the word mean anyway? The tiny steps I was taking in this newfound world of mine still had a lot to teach me but one truth I had already learnt was that this path of faith demanded patience and perseverance in abundance. On recognising this, I prayed to Him for both in equal proportions! Life taught me to commit myself to something that I couldn't change, like my DNA.

8

The Unbreakable Threads of Karma

> Man is an embodiment of his karma.
> He embodies the virtues of simplicity, purity
> and spirituality, and in the same vein
> he embodies complexity, dirt and evil.
>
> *Anonymous*

I often wished that I had the ways and means to recover the book of my life and my many lifetimes to see where I had erred and how I could possibly rectify my mistakes to redeem my life. 'Can I turn back the clock so that I could do it differently?' To be given one more chance is the futile plea of most. 'Life is the art of drawing without an eraser,' reminds us John W Gardner. But while most of us know this, we do not draw our lines properly!

Life is an accumulation of errors, and the blunders of my past are repaying me in the present and how. The law of cause and effect is strict and exact but when I try and recollect my mistakes, I honestly do not feel that the sum total of my misery is in direct proportion to the misery I may have caused others. There seems to be an error in my balance sheet! Math was never my all-time favourite, so now that I have my Guruji, I prefer to leave my life's equation for Him to figure out as who could be more skilled an accountant than Him? I would, however, like to suggest that You, Guruji, subtract my marital discord to multiply my joys and add value to my life! This would return a measure of my dignity and tranquillity back to me. I am quite certain that you, the greatest mathematician in the world, will be greatly impressed by my formula for my happiness and, more importantly, for my sound health and that supreme state of mind where peace reigns. I began giving out love and patience in my marriage as well as acceptance, hoping that the reward will come back with mathematical precision.

Guruji summoned me to the front, where His resonant voice blessed me with words uttered emphatically, 'I have tried and tested you ceaselessly, squeezed you like a lemon and now go and see your reflection without switching off the bathroom light!!'

This happened after several months of being with Him, loving him, arguing with Him, resenting Him and finally accepting Him and His word without a question. Yet, many, such as I, could never totally surrender to His word. The vessel of my wisdom and understanding was very narrow and shallow. How can a vessel ever fill with His wisdom when the lid is never completely taken off? We always leave the light on in our logical minds even after entering the space of faith and devotion.

'Switch on your bathroom light and see your reflection and each time you do, be grateful. An attitude of gratitude will fetch you many more blessings,' reassured Guruji. 'Always imagine me standing behind you, as when you, do I will appear. Very few are fortunate enough to believe. Hence, they fail to receive. Live your life either believing or live it rejecting. The choices are always yours and the consequences of your choices are always mine.' He uttered these words whilst staring at me directly and I lowered my gaze to His feet. Then I gently closed my eyes. Only He fathomed the depth of my emotions. That moment far exceeded the ordinary and I was silenced. Even my ever-chattering mind where silence never reigns became quiet momentarily. Truly, very few of us experience life-changing moments and this was mine to cherish.

'You cannot change certain circumstances as they are pre-ordained and are set in accordance with your karma. You cannot change the seasons, the wind or the rain but you can change yourself. That is something you have charge of and the rest, you will have to leave to me. That is called 'surrender' but very few have the wisdom to understand its depth. Do you, Anita? I am here to give but very few know how to receive the real thing. They are ensnared in their petty desires that are trivial in nature. Learn to take that blessing which is to your benefit in the larger scheme of things. Ask and it shall be given.'

Wisdom? I didn't know what the word meant but what I did clearly encounter was a sea change in the way my skin was healing miraculously. At first, it turned from red to pink, the pus reduced, as did the blood and the severe flakiness to make it appear less nasty. The rashes on the body also reduced but didn't disappear altogether. The severe itchiness also calmed down and didn't misbehave as badly as it did previously. Only He knew, and God knows how, that I switched off my bathroom light before entering it out of sheer apprehension of catching a glimpse of myself, the eyesore. In all my knowing, I now knew that He was omnipresent, hence, more than a mere Guru with healing powers.

Over the next several months, my skin turned pale pink before it became normal. Within a year of His blessings, I had a fairly healthy looking skin that made me look fairly attractive! I could gaze into the mirror comfortably without being daunted by the reflection. In some capacity, it was too good to be true. Who could have believed it as even my own mind questioned the phenomenon even after having witnessed the change on a daily basis.

Faith is irrational, illogical, unreasonable, unimaginable and unintelligent as well as ridiculously absurd and brainless, to put it simply! As for my questioning mind, it is a daily decision to stay with faith and to befriend it further, as my entire existence depends on it. The nature of faith, however, is such that because it has a mind of its own, it is sometimes steadfast, then at other times, shaky. Unpredictable! But then the name of the game was to manoeuvre myself gently back onto the path.

After many more months, a certain acceptance of my circumstances did come about and I no longer resisted it awhile. A measure of serenity permeated my being and I almost ceased to question my sealed fate. I just about made peace with it as I believed that I had been granted a new lease of life, literally. I had very nearly transcended my situation, rising above its abnormalities. Born of the hopelessness of my situation was something larger and greater than what I could understand. What was definite is that I was able to connect to my finer, higher feelings that would distract me from the mainstream ones for a while. Perhaps Guruji had taught me to separate myself from my external environment to connect me deeper to my internal life.

'If I had not healed you of your skin cancer and asthma, you would have passed on, as you were at the end of your life's road. I was compelled to heal you and in due course, you will understand the reason for the same. Now there is no need to consult astrologers, as by doing so, you interfere with my work as he foresees with his limited vision whilst I change your stars to re-write your destiny. Who then is more accurate? No one except your Guruji came forward to reach out to you, Anita. In your hour of distress, neither your mother, nor father, nor brother nor friend came forward. Only your Guruji is all-compassion and all-serving to his disciple. When I bless you and your relationships, then they too become smooth,' said Guruji on a day when I sat quietly with Him, sipping my customary blessed tea but this time in His private room where few were blessed to enter, a privilege I was eternally grateful for. He had related this to me in the winter of 1998. Of course, at that time, I failed to comprehend the reason for this enormous benediction but His words did ring true as they corresponded precisely with those of an astrologer I had visited in 1997 who had sympathised with my birth chart and stated hesitatingly that there was no life beyond that year. It was the same astrologer who had summoned me to give him ₹15,000 so that he could pray for me. Cute! And now I wanted to pray for him and his well-being. After being blessed, I wanted the entire population of planet earth to come to Guruji to seek His blessings. For me, at this point in my life, anyone who did not worship Guruji was an oddball and wasn't living his or her life fully!

Although the canvas of my home remained pretty much unchanged, it is I who began to change. My attitude became moderately hopeful and optimistic and although things were no better in reality, I just felt better about them. I had began to earn a measure of self-respect too as I tolerated less misconduct than before. I knew the divine engineer was working on my internal mechanics as I was becoming stronger and sturdier. The silent blessings that are often not spelt out by Him go unheeded but on some level, they could be felt. I felt the emotion of self-love rising within and my self-worth was beginning to flex the muscle to climb over the Berlin Wall! Since I had recovered from my physical traumas, I was better able to manage my emotional ones. Since regaining my health, the quality of my life improved radically and that naturally spilled over in my relationship with my daughters, Anishka and Sonakshi, who were growing to be fiercely intelligent and cultured. That was incredibly satisfying and rewarding to observe. That they had Guruji's divine protection was clear to see and things were happening for them on their own. Their strong personalities commanded respect and they earned it through their shining performances at school making the grade in all their subjects. I was a proud mother and meeting their teachers on parents' evenings was a delight, as on my arrival, they would smile and state that they are both performing well but the only grievance they had was that they were so good that on finishing their course early, they would start chattering and distracting the rest of the class. Yep! That sure sounded like my yapping girls who had too much to say. My hands-on motherhood to both my dolls also gave me unbounded personal fulfillment and essentially they remained the reason for my tolerance in the marriage.

My secret mantra, however, was still the same. It was such a deep secret that I no longer vocalised it to Guruji anymore.

And I always remember the Christian prayer: 'Where there is darkness, there is light'

9

Buddhism

The light of spirituality encompasses all faiths.

Anonymous

My spiritual path widened as I turned to reading extensively and earnestly, perhaps to internalise certain truths about my purpose and the reason for having chosen such an arduous journey. I did believe then and I am still convinced that it was my soul that demanded the experiences that I attracted into my life for its evolution and growth. Pain is an evolutionary journey and it need not be taken as eternal suffering, as we can end it with our free will. Also, it is truly in the dark that we begin to seek light. The suffering ends when the realisation begins and somewhere along the way, I ceased to play the blame game and took responsibility for my own actions and reactions. I became a prolific reader of Brian Weiss, Eckhart Tolle, Louise Hay, Neale Walsch and James Redfield. It's difficult to single out any particular one who I fell deeply in love with. I began an affair with all of them and each of them taught me something about myself.

I must not fail to acknowledge that even after embracing Guruji as my saviour and guide and knowing full well that He healed me, I turned to Buddhism to intellectualise the law of cause and effect. The reason for this was self-empowerment through understanding the universal laws. One of the prime ones was the law of oneness of self and environment. This understanding was priceless for me, as by changing my inner scenery that reflected the outer, I could make that shift. The hues of strength and fortitude had to be applied on my internal landscape for me to attract healthier and happier situations. Through this knowledge, my thoughts morphed into something deeper that kindled a sense of mission in me to change from within. 'Be the change you want to see,' said Mahatma Gandhi and we are all familiar with this truth: we cannot change others but we can most certainly change ourselves. What certainly was brought home to me was the fact that even on visiting a doctor for a malady, he gives us pills that are to be taken only by us for our internal malady and not by anyone else. When we want change, then our reactions, actions, perceptions and responses to ourselves must change first for us to see the change outside of ourselves. Our self-image must grow for us to no longer shrink in a debilitating situation. Our limiting beliefs need to alter too for us to live with unlimited love and self-respect that will attract that and more into our lives.

In the depths of my ignorant self, I was bearing a grudge against my Guruji as I thought that He hadn't got a grip of my domestic situation. I pleaded with the being that had become my 'all' overnight, my most revered and loved Guruji, to sanction my divorce. Yet, He declined through and through. I implored repeatedly but in vain. I felt that He no longer empathised with my condition and even though I had accepted my lot, I believed that I deserved a measure of self-respect and maybe an ounce of happiness which I was not receiving here. There is a vast difference between acceptance and true happiness. I longed for the latter. Somewhere in the dense forest of faith, my grip with Guruji loosened awhile as I felt He had become indifferent to my matrimonial issues.

Buddhism enabled me to grasp the law of cause and effect on a very deep level. I became a leader in a hurry and began to encourage others to take charge of their lives. I was totally involved and actively participated in group studies and activities. I felt a deep sense of purpose as my understanding began to grow by leaps and bounds. I was happy as I brought about changes in other's lives through my own inner changes. I almost became a beacon of light for other members. Very soon, I earned a large measure of respect and admiration. I savoured the adulation, the awe and the growing awareness. I began to feel empowered, as my own domestic situation no longer disempowered me. Both my spiritual paths ran parallel as I would successfully engage myself in Buddhist activities during the day and visit Guruji in the evenings, perhaps once a week or fortnight, as it was instructed by Him. Initially, he had ordered me to visit Him every day without exception. His word was law and I never refuted it but I failed to speak to Him about my Buddhist practice for fear that He would discourage me. In hindsight, I realise that He knew all along but never objected because I needed to ascertain my path through the deviation and, perhaps, understand and appreciate it better. We learn through contrasts and time is the most adept teacher.

See it as digression or a temporary departure from my real path, for me it was an education, as through the volumes of books I read and discussed with other members, I understood chapter and verse of my own life. A rich intellectual life is synonymous with a rich spiritual life. The inner life determines the outer.

I also realised that my dependence on Guruji's physical presence grew much more than He wanted, as often He would suggest for me to go within. 'You must start meditating as then you will become one with the 'uni-verse' (one-song).'

God helps those who help themselves and I was not helping myself, neither through prayer nor action. There is no denying that there was an internal growth that happened through Buddhism that was probably a rung on my ladder of evolution. I understood myself better and also gained much more clarity on Guruji and my relationship with Him. I also gained more clarity on my relationship with my husband only to realise that I was to stop blaming myself for the abuse that was coming my way by deeply respecting my life. In addition, the practice brought home the fact that I could not sue anyone for the things that went wrong in my own life. Taking ownership of my thoughts, words and deeds and accepting responsibility to change the negative into positive had almost become my mission. By now, I was only mildly angry at life and that too was mostly overridden by my determination to bring about change.

Somewhere along my path of spirituality, I learned to see things for what they were and have the courage and wisdom to do what was ethically right, No matter how much so-called love it comes with or is compensated with, in hindsight, abuse is totally and unmistakably wrong. It is base behaviour that should not be condoned, no matter what the situation and it certainly should not be romanticised! It is inexcusable, no matter what the excuses for its provocation and someone who loves you will most certainly not mistreat you. On the contrary, he will lift you and not bring you down. The justification that, 'He is under pressure. Hence, he loses it' or 'He is good at heart but doesn't know how to show it' are feeble attempts at sugar-coating abuse. First, recognise the truth, then act on it. In addition, you cannot go on playing the game of life by blaming others but by taking total responsibility for your actions and reactions. To sum it up, having the courage of your convictions, standing up for yourself, and not bowing and cowering to abase behaviour is what will eventually put a stop to it. I am a firm believer that internal strength can be gained only through spirituality, which raises our frequency, allowing us to attract only the good whilst it filters out the bad.

Life mirrors back precisely what we send out to it. The laws of attraction were working in my life very evidently. My intentions were as clear as day. I wanted a life clear of maltreatment and manipulation, to create an environment which was healthy not only for myself but for my growing daughters who I wanted to see blossom with healthy thoughts on men-and-women relationships. It was imperative for them to perceive me as a strong sturdy mother who lived her life with self-respect and healthy self-esteem versus a mother devoid of those attributes. My desire to be an idol to my daughters was far stronger than my desire to win a self-deprecating battle that each time gave me the title of a self-sacrificing martyr.

With my every prayer came the affirmation, 'I am living in a healthy and happy environment with my blossoming daughters. I believe I am worthy of love and respect and I am surrounded by it here and now. So be it.' I ceased to look at 'control' and 'manipulation' through rose-tinted spectacles. Guruji had given me the courage to no longer sugar-coat my unsavoury situation even though I believed at the time that He didn't approve of my exit. Regardless of the profuse apologies as well as the regrets from my counterpart, the game of control became ever so clear and I became ever more determined not play it any longer. I knew for certain that I would sooner rather than later turn my back on my marriage for the right reasons— to take my daughters and I onto the right course. Divorce is not what a woman signs up for when she takes her wedding vows that are meant to be for life but when what we dream of is frequently at odds with our reality, then a practical decision needs to be taken. I needed incalculable prayers to break the stiff knots of my karma. It was vitally important for me to take a courageous stance of breaking the heartbreaking news to my orthodox, in-the-box parents, living under the lock and key of their own conditioning and time-honoured values. They naturally viewed divorce as an earth-shattering proposal. I knew as I had experienced earlier that they would not take too kindly to my decision but this time, I had the resolve of a warrior and nothing and no one was going to bring down my defenses. If you are to win over any of your life's battle, then you have to 'be in it to win it'.

When I willingly gave up the Buddhist chanting, I once again embraced my Guru's mantra which was '*Om Namah Shivay, Guruji Sada Sahay*'. I would chant this mantra collectively with other disciples and when alone in my quieter moments. It gave me strength and endurance that could not be quantified. This mantra became an intrinsic part of me along with His passport-sized photos that fit comfortably in my every handbag and often in the pocket of my jeans! I just needed to make sure that He walked me through my ordeal to guide and guard me. I believed that's the least He could do, considering He refused to support me with vitamin D (divorce) and instead supplemented me with vitamin E (endurance) and like how!

My shoes still did not fit and every day I silently acknowledged this truth to myself. They were as uncomfortable as ever and I simply could not be in denial of this ugly truth anymore, hence, the affirmations, the mantra for inner fortitude and my silent pleas to the higher forces. I just wasn't willing to give up the fist fight with my karma to win back my dignity. My latent internal freedom awaited it to be given expression whilst I remained in the shackles of the external confines. Happiness, at this point, seemed like a real stretch of the imagination. Yet, there were subtle signs of a shift taking place. The soul traverses many experiences before coming back home and it is the invincibility of the spirit that carries us back to where we belong. I knew in the depth and breadth of my being that my situation was going to be water under the bridge in times to come. Challenges make life interesting; however, overcoming them is what makes life meaningful.

10

The Rebirth on His Birthday

*I am an optimist and I assume God is too.
Otherwise He would have
kicked us off this planet and started over long ago!*

Anonymous

Beyond a point, it is up to us to take the initiative instead of
waiting for situations to present themselves. It is a positively
liberating experience to recognise what is good for us in the long
term, then forge ahead. No individual or force can sentence us to
a lifetime of unhappiness and self-denial unless we choose that
for ourselves.

I had immersed myself for way too long in l-if-e's 'what if '
and 'if only.' Life had almost passed me by in my thinking about
my liberation from the wrong until push came to shove and life
forced me out of the situation like a gush of strong wind, perhaps
more accurately, a hurricane! Hence, the shoes that didn't fit were

thrown out by life, finally. The universe really did conspire to bring the good forces together to help me take off my shoes and misfit coat that I so knew I had to bid farewell to. It took years to do so—18 to be precise.

The dictates of the conditioning of my mind coupled with my cultivated fears and self-doubts prevented me from breaking the shackles. It is often easier to remain imprisoned to discomfort that you become so ridiculously comfortable with than go down the unbeaten road. Accepting powerlessness is sometimes an easier option than mustering one's courage to gain power over the unknown. The world out there can be a potentially frightening place, like running into a snake pit, particularly if you haven't been exposed to it before. My father supported me in my growing years before my husband took over. Economic dependence is what compels most broken-spirited women to endure life-long assaults of 'you-are-a-good-for-nothing' that eventually reduce you to nothing. Words are the only weightless thing in the world that heavily weighs you down. I was held so mercilessly captive by the limits of my own imagination and foresight as well as my negative self-belief that I spiralled down over time. In a perverse sense, I also stayed because I was unrealistically optimistic about things getting better. That delusion was lifted some time back although it lasted for well over a decade.

Personal power comes at the most unexpected hour and is independent of outside approval, opinion or consent. It also crosses the boundaries of your conditioning and conservative upbringing. It comes from within ourselves like a tornado that propels us forward. You acknowledge the thorn in your side with honesty, then you pull it out with a force you never knew existed. My! How the universe conspires and cooperates with you, to make that which you need more than anything else in the world, happen. It's almost like the universe finally gives in to your resolve. 'No!' Says the universe to begin with and insists on its 'No!' The individual persists and says, 'Yes!' The inner resolve to do what must be done carries on unrelentingly. It is so tenacious that 'Yes' becomes its silent affirmation and one fine day, the silent resolve becomes obstinate enough for the universe to give in!

On 7th July, 2006, two days after I had carefully walked out of my marriage with a determination I had never known or felt before, I walked into my Guruji's temple to inform Him of my exit. Take note of my carefully chosen word 'inform' and not 'inquire.' I had been in the UK until 5th July from the month of June and it was immediately on arriving on Indian soil that I walked out after long and careful deliberation and an extended dialogue with my parents. During my stay in Manchester, I had received a call from Bamby who of course was a staunch Guruji devotee. She insisted that I come back to Guruji as He needed to bless me. She insisted that He knew what I had done! I disregarded the call and instead, on my eight-hour flight, I spent six hours chanting for my exit to be a smooth sail. No one besides my family knew of my walking out, so there was no way in which Guruji could have been informed within two days of my return as my family was not in touch with Him. At that point, none of my family members had really taken to Him. Sanjeev, my youngest brother, had visited him a few times intermittently but he was not in regular touch with Him, not yet anyway.

It was in January 2006 that I made my resolution to become indomitable. My silent courage that spoke only to me knew that I would need to make that exit. For a while, I ceased to visit Guruji's darbar. I felt that He might weaken my resolve. In my ignorance, I avoided the people and place remotely connected with Guruji. My courage was silently roaring and I couldn't even stop myself from surging forward. I was unstoppable and I was certain that the tide was about to turn.

I wore an attitude of ingratitude towards my Guru as I inched towards Him with my head held high and my shoulders back and upright. My body language very audibly stated 'I no longer care about karmic right or wrong. I am truly done with the spiritual mumbo jumbo of karmic retribution and dialogues like "There's a time for everything" and "It's your lot" and "It's all you've got, so bear it with a grin".' Nothing was going to change my determined mind and resolute heart. I was prepared to listen to only my inner voice in all its wisdom, and what it told me. My intentions were not to seek His grace and blessings for a divorce as He had rejected my plea time and again. I had urged Him on more than one occasion to break my marriage karma but He had flatly refused. I had resented Him awhile and I began to believe that perhaps I did not deserve happiness. In the same breath, He mocked me and ridiculed me by insisting that my father make me secure. He asked me not to repeat my surname to people I introduced myself to. I failed to understand Him and His intentions, as He did not spell anything out to me. I grudgingly resigned to my destiny until I felt strong and began to believe that I was worthy of breathing healthy air. I was convinced that what I demanded was a dignified desire of the heart for self-preservation and self-respect. No more.

As I arrogantly began to take my strides towards Him for a formal bow, as it was His birthday and I merely came as a mark of respect and gratitude for healing me of my health issues, He called out to me and very audibly before hundreds of others He exclaimed, 'Divorce, divorce, divorce and now you will realise true happiness.' My eyes widened as I glared at Him out of shock! I fell helplessly and humbly at His feet, then looked up at Him skeptically. 'You are not kidding me, are you?' I thought. 'You are in no way mocking me, right?' I thought again. Then I mustered up courage to ask out aloud as I frowned 'Guruji? Are you sure?'

All these years, He had been denying me my most dignified and rightful longing. I yearned for freedom from my suffocation. Above all else, I needed peace of mind that I had been brutally deprived of. I had been starved of the basic human desire to be loved, nurtured and appreciated. I was stripped of my respect and yet, He, my Guru who had granted me a new life, new skin, new pair of lungs and probably new cells, tissues, fibres, new kidneys along with a new heart and just about every piece of my anatomy, was unable to grant me peace. My heart was breaking as it was paining and He could do nothing about it. What was the point in giving me new lungs without giving me the air to breathe? They were half-baked blessings and I only half-heartedly accepted them as there was a strong missing link. All His blessings seemed inconsequential and insignificant without the freedom of real happiness. There was nothing to write home about, not until that momentous, vitally life-changing moment.

My heart was singing and my spirit was dancing. I was elated and ecstatic beyond measure. As I knelt before Him, I gazed up at Him, my eyes shining with adoration and devotion, yet with an element of disbelief. I wondered if in the next moment, He would say 'Sucker! I made a fool out of you! I was just kidding mate! No divorce for you! Your fate is sealed, so just accept your lot and go home and do what you've always done. My blessings are always with you for your eternal make-believe happiness in your unhappy situation. Now go and live unhappily ever after!'

I waited at His feet for something to change as skepticism and its ugly sister cynicism had become a part of me and I barely believed in life anymore. There were ripples of fear and a slight current of disturbance within me fused with a wave of joy as the tide really had turned. I still had my head bowed as I sat still with bated breath and a fluttering sensation in the pit of my stomach. He gazed at me with compassion-filled eyes and then urged me to leave after giving me a reassuring smile and commanding me to come and visit Him on another day. This long-awaited moment sent a chill down my spine as it was completely unforeseen.

'Go home and sit in silence. Chant the Shiva mantra for strength, as you will need it. Go and live your life with joy, love, respect and much more. In a word, live again. Love again and feel again. Take care of your daughters. Love them and protect them from the pain that they are feeling. Your father and brothers will now get together to give you their full support. Remember, emotionally it will not be easy to begin with, so be strong and wise. I am with you. Have faith. *Om Namah Shivay Shivji Sada Sahay, Om Namah Shivay Guruji Sada Sahay.'*

My eyes welled up with tears but my heart and soul were laughing joyously, celebrating with champagne and hors d'oeuvres! I felt the rapture within my heart and soul as they did the salsa! Music filled every inch of my being, dancing like never before. I felt the joy of being alive, the simple act of inhaling the air deeply and delightfully. As I waltzed out of the haven of His temple, I observed the well-manicured lawns adorned with fully blossomed roses and dahlias on either side. All my senses were alive and I observed all that I was previously blind to. I inhaled the aroma too, filling my lungs satisfactorily like a woman in love. 'Oms' had been meticulously carved within the bushes and hedges by His blessed gardener. The landscape of the temple boasted abundant nature and stunning beauty and grandeur. How come I had never noticed the purity and poetry of the temple earlier? Claude Monet could not have painted this better with all its colour, tones, textures fringed with rapturous emotions. The spirit of it simply could not be captured on camera, canvas or any other gadget, instrument or material. It was so awe inspiring that every skeptic became a believer on entering the vicinity of the temple that Guruji Himself had constructed for His disciples of today and for those in times to come. He had clearly stated that this temple was equivalent to the 12 most powerful shrines in the world and anyone who came here with pure faith and positive surrender would be blessed. The winning card was 'surrender' and even though there were always more questions than answers, it was best to play blind in the game of faith. He had stated that His following would grow by leaps and bounds in years to come and there would be a mile-long queue outside the temple of people waiting to seek his blessings. He also declared that sooner rather than later, His sublime light would permeate every nook and corner of the world. Guruji was the architect who had visualised, conceptualised and actualised this unique temple. Needless to say, He was and is the architect of my happiness. He is the builder of hope and faith who cements these with the promise of eternal love and salvation. If it weren't for His eternal grace, I would've still been drowning in the ocean of despair and dejection. I recall arriving at His doorstep parched and He with His immeasurable mercy, gave me more than a measure of His love to quench my thirst. I dread to think what would have happened if He too had turned His back on me in the same way that I had turned mine. Thank goodness He had more sense than I ever will!

The magical beauty of the temple was for all to enjoy. Since it was built away from the commotion of the city, people recharged their souls in the silence of their bodily temple whilst soaking in His benign grace through every pore of the skin. It was to be assimilated by all the human senses. It was to be felt and internalised. The unreal cannot substitute the real and the real beauty was that each individual had access to it. The password was faith and once you logged in, the unending quest began and logging out was an option very few took.

The Shivalinga sat invincibly on the roof of the temple and the Shiva statue in the midst of the fountain, which was encompassed by lotus-shaped marble, seemed to be smiling at me as I bowed to it in deep reverence and overwhelming joy. The smile on my face was fixed, glued with the supernatural and all-powerful glue! I smiled at all the people who passed me by at the temple. Most of them were unfamiliar to me. I smiled at them anyway and they reciprocated though they were unaware of the reason for my jubilation. Each individual revelled in his or her own joyfulness, barring the odd disgruntled disciple whose faith was probably being tested by Guruji. He, like most of us, wanted a quick-fix for his problems. Most people are afraid to make the flight as it requires breaking the habits and patterns that govern our behaviour, actions and reactions. The pre-requisite to blessings is faith but then for some it is blessings first, faith later. 'You scratch my back and I'll scratch yours!' is their undercover deal.

It was since 1997 that I was pleading with Him for a divorce. It was finally in 2006 that He blessed me with it. As I understood it, there were no cutting corners in the realm of faith and I simply needed to go through the process for Him cutting my karma. The conviction and commitment, espoused with the confidence that He is sowing the seeds that will bear the most desirable fruit, equal surrender. Of course, at this point in my journey, I was on shaky ground, void of the attributes that require steady and steadfast devotion, so my growth, I believe, was rather slow but Guruji was keeping me steady. Moliere was right: 'The trees that are slow to grow bear the best fruits.'

I then looked up at the skies and saw similar brush strokes that I had seen as a 12 year old. It all appeared so beautiful, the clear skies untainted with mist and haze and the crisp air unpolluted with people's enduring skepticism and suspicion of the unseen power that lay in the temple. Beyond doubt, God is the artist who alters the canvas of our lives when we sincerely believe. I once again drew in His aroma of roses that soaked the air inside and outside the temple. He had set the tone for me to fall in love again with life. The place pulsated with irresistible love and supreme joy as I too throbbed with the very same energy. I glowed like a light bulb as I continued to beam intensely at the sheer thought of being alive and becoming one with the universe. Was I glad for this moment! I had an uncontrollable urge to scream on top of my lungs the words 'I love you Guruji and Thaaaaank you.' As love and gratitude permeated me, I skipped out of the temple, deeply inhaling the salubrious air, with a piece of music in my heart and a rhythm in my feet that was all too familiar to me only as a teenager. I marvelled at the jaw-dropping sight of the temple once again from the outside with its entire splendour. Then I marvelled at my good karma that had introduced me to Guruji. I may have suffered but through it and because of it, I met God! Darkness truly becomes an illusion when light takes over.

On the auspicious day of Gurujis birthday, 7th July, the temple is adorned with abundant roses, colourful flowers, and neon lights across the entire place including the lawns. Mellifluous shabads reverberate in the air and the delicious aroma of the heartwarming food that is medicine is served as a buffet on account of the enormity of the crowd. The disciples queue up for the blessed food that is served virtually all night long and I for one, rate it higher than any other meal I have ever had outside the temple. What more can we ask for when the food is both sacred and scrumptious?

I had been blessed tonight without assimilating the additional blessings of food and drink and for reasons known only to Guruji. He chose not to allow me to stay for the all-night celebrations that included live music and folk dance by a renowned Punjabi group from Punjab. The resounding euphoria, I knew, would last through the night as free-spirited people would later get up and dance till the break of dawn. The celebrations filled the air with His divinity and with the devotion of the disciples who urged the night not to end even though they knew very well that their joy and jubilation would go on long after it was all over.

He looked splendid in His richly embroidered attire and His beaming face that smiled compassionately at His disciples whilst blessing them at a very deep level without their awareness. We all want a sign, a tangible verification of Guruji's ability to make that needful shift in our lives, bringing about a change that will afford us happiness, but sometimes Guruji works on the soul level and our logical, reasoning minds feel disillusioned as they needs to *see* the change with.

'I love you Guruji,' I heard myself say over and over and over again in a never-ending beat 'I love you so-so-so much!'

I was full of beans and self-pride as not only had I mustered up the courage to take the plunge but I had also received the divine blessings of my beloved Guruji as well as blessings of my father, my mother, my brothers, my friends, acquaintances and well-wishers. I felt that the entire universe had blessed me. The heavens, the moon, the stars and all the planets and the people there, if at all there was life there, smiled down at me and congratulated me! I looked at my situation directly in the eye and with conviction and a firm resolute voice, said, 'ENOUGH! I need it no more.' I had made my bed many years before but I no longer needed to lie in it. As I have understood it, life is a never-ending metamorphosis. It is always changing, always transforming and through the continuous stream of experiences, we are constantly meeting ourselves. Hence, we are also always changing. I viewed this as the END—entirely new direction. It was all good, as I was blessed to have been given a second chance to 'start all over again.'

I had philosophically and spiritually analysed the pages of my life to grasp the reasons for all its occurrences. I knew I had learned life's lessons and I now needed to take another road, the high road, the one with many inroads of peace, prosperity and unbounded pleasure. Isn't that what most mere mortals like me wanted out of life anyway?

The soul needs to go through the rain, sleet, snow and storm to come out on the other side, dry and smiling!

11

My Eternal Friend

There is something stronger than us, something higher and more powerful and, of course, inexplicable.

Anonymous

My Guruji cast off His physical body on 31st May 2007. He was an enigma and His sudden disappearance, a mystery. Immediately after He left, I continued to visit His temple with no lesser devotion, love and belief except I deeply missed our union. I was disturbed but not distraught by his departure, as I believed in His omnipresence hereafter.

A week before He departed from the earth plane, He cleared a few misinterpretations of mine that I had formed in my ignorance. It was a Thursday evening and at 11 pm He, with His gracious lyrical gesture and glance, motioned His devotees to leave while He gently asked me to sit beside Him. He then stated, 'It is not easy to embrace your Guru's love as it demands total surrender.

I gave you what you wanted and needed in the right time, space and sequence. When you first came to me, you were too sick to stand upright, Yet, you foolishly asked me for a divorce! How did you propose to stand with dignity in society when there was very little of your life left? I gave you both life and life-force. I strengthened you from within whilst strengthening your bank balance! I knew I had to grant you a divorce but you were fast losing faith in me and in my script for you. I was always with you even when you felt me no more beside you. I am and will always be with you. Feel me in your heart and truly surrender to me. Go and live your life.' I listened attentively with my head bowed and He continued after a moment's pause, 'Go back to England and initiate satsangs. Now you may go. I have made you a leader and someday you will marry again!'

All three declarations by the divine being were abstract to my mind and not relatable. I missed the chance to discuss my desire not to leave the country after having fallen in love with it and my deeper desire of never marrying again after having fallen out of love with the mere thought of it!

I bowed to Him to leave Him believing that I would visit Him again in a few days. As I bowed to Him, I telepathically declared, 'I love you,' to which He immediately responded vocally, 'I love you too!' And that was perhaps the last time I was to hear Him say those words to me but it was not my last embrace as I knew that He had sealed my fate with His divine kiss.

In hindsight, He had cleared my vision. I went over the sequence of events, His statements and the final blessings only to realise that He was indeed preparing me for my exit and then the life after. He had blessed me with a calm, courageous and confident self. He granted me my physical and emotional stability, then my financial security and finally deepened my spirituality to impart to me a practical understanding of my life. He had blessed me on every front in the real practical sense. This is testimony of Guruji's Supremacy as the avatar of kalyug (age of discord) who descended on earth to uplift humanity, to realign peoples' values, to regenerate their morals and to remind them that there is a dire need for a shift of consciousness, and it is through collective prayer and practical changes that real happiness and peace can be attained.

Guruji seldom preached. On the contrary, He ensured that people who came to Him lived fully with complete understanding of their lives to be better human beings who live simply, keeping the theory of karma in mind. The verification of His divinity came through our personal experiences and through those who were there before us and who shared their knowledge and experiences as well. We draw value from each other. On His insistence, a devotee would visit Him regularly for Him to bring about an inner and outer change in his/her life whilst He worked on the soul level before all the other levels. The receptivity of His devotees made it easier for Him to do His work and people who came to Him with doubt and negative thinking towards Him blocked their own energy centres disallowing him to reconstruct their broken, fragmented lives. Our negative thinking is the Berlin Wall of concrete doubt and cynicism. The high walls that we build around us become impermeable and disallow the light of divinity to filter in. Going to Guruji as empty vessels, leaving behind our egos, preconceived notions and beliefs as well as our mostly warped conditioning enables Him to fill us with His light. After more than a decade, I realised that He is the master gardener of our lives who knew what weeds to take out and what seeds to sow into our lives to flower with our patience and perseverance. Faith is the only water that can quench our thirst. The other illusory and delusional pleasures of the world leave us thirsty for more. In that sense, every other pleasure is insatiable. Addictions and cravings are a consequence of the lack of fulfillment of those pleasures one time, so we indulge in them endlessly without ever attaining any lasting satisfaction.

I recall one Wednesday morning after His physical departure, there were possibly eight or nine disciples in the temple to conduct seva (selfless devotional work) such as sweeping and washing the floor, cleaning the inside of the temple, polishing it and later, adorning Guruji's seat with bouquets of flowers, roses and garlands followed by the lighting of the diya (candle) and the incense sticks. I observed their staunch devotion and unconditional love while they sang 'Om Namah Shivay…' harmoniously as they went about performing their duties with utmost pleasure. They were enviably happy and the radiance on their faces was a true indication of their fondest love for their Lord.

Guruji had bestowed on these men and women an inner serenity that I so longed for. I, for one, sat by myself on the lawn that was lush and verdant while a gentle breeze encompassed the entire place that was still unspoiled and unsoiled; it was as entrancing as ever, as though Guruji were still managing the place through His beloved disciples. With their unrivalled love and devotion, they would maintain its pristine state, as it was a heavenly abode where they came to surrender their difficulties. It was their powerhouse and they visited it regularly to charge and revitalise their spirits, and gain spiritual command.

It was October end. I was away from the challenges of my everyday existence. Instead, I engaged my mind with the sights and sounds of the temple, away from the city's clamour. If you've ever visited Delhi, you will know that the city is suffocated with noise and air pollution and choked with traffic. Particularly at this festive time of the year with Diwali in the air, fireworks light up the sky in flashes of red, yellow, green and maroon. It's incredible how a festival can transform an entire city, altering its rhythm and mood. With Indian hospitality at its peak, the air crackles with merriments and high-spiritedness. Bright-eyed people shower each other with endearments and goodwill as their paths cross and relatives make their frenetic rounds to visit their extended families to offer gifts, sweets and greetings. Even the grudging relatives smile as it's the time of the year to forgive, forget and get! Daytime is warm but in the cool of the evening, just as twilight begins, the streets and mall squares awaken to the effervescence of the festivities. Public places are inundated with beaming faces that joyfully wear their collective anticipation of a celebration that open up hearts and chokes the air. The old city of Delhi is even more chaotic with artisans, traders and business people unified in the spirit of Diwali, the most animated celebration of lights.

Guruji's temple was a contrast, a true heaven on earth where tranquility reigned supreme and people came to unclog their lives and clear the pollution of their troubled minds. Their energy and mood transformed for the time that they either sat in quiet reflection or actively engaged themselves in seva. After a point, however, their entire lives became a celebration with their faces beaming with the same joy and their eyes shining with the excitement of having received a gift for life. A visit to Guruji's ashram is likened to imbibing all the holy books in 3 hours without having to read them! The wisdom permeates us without any effort besides simply being in that space and connecting to Him. I understood in one single experience that my voracious appetite in childhood to read the *Gita* was now satisfied in the here and now.

There were several ways of connecting with Him but my interaction with other disciples as well as my involvement with group seva were minimal unless I was asked to do satsang which in time did become frequent, almost every time! This suited my personality as I had the gift of the gab and each time I would speak, I would draw more and more people who listened attentively and were inspired. In time, my life became a message of hope and faith for others. Guruji had clearly willed it before He discarded His physical garb. His hukum was for me to do satsangs everywhere, and not just here in Delhi. So later, I began to travel the world over to share my blessings. Act as if what you do makes a difference. It does.

My desire to elevate others elevated me. Also what came home to me was the fact that human struggle, strife and suffering are the same everywhere. We are part of a collective destiny of a shared humanity and our issues are just dressed differently. My own struggles sensitised me to theirs and each time I observed a ray of hope in people's eyes, I spoke with more gusto and had more generosity to share. I was careful, however, not to get myself entwined in the personal lives of others and their complex issues, as I was not the healer but a mere mortal who had been blessed sufficiently to understand certain forgotten truths. Besides, Guruji had indicated to me more than once that I am not strong enough to take on board others negativity. Hence, I am careful to live in line with His will. I share my experiences as He blesses the one who shares and the one who listens. I stress the importance of visiting the temple regularly for the canvas of people's lives to change. Arriving at the temple, assimilating the shabad, consuming the relishing, sacred langar that is revealing of a power that cannot be savoured by the taste buds and imbibing His aura that prevails more than ever, are the ingredients that heal from lifetimes of karma.

Guruji was and is the one who blesses and He had repeatedly instructed me to inject faith in others, as it was not only the need of the day but the sharing of experiences is also an expression of Guruji love through one or many individuals. He is healing people through our satsangs as He has blessed those expressions. His energy permeates the place as well as the people as His divine energy has no physical limitations and He blesses indiscriminately. In these times of instability at every level, He is our stability. Hence, today's people are receptive to the ancient truths and they respond well to Guruji being the modern avatar. 'Yes,' some respond, 'Every era needs an avatar to uplift humanity and save it from the destruction of its own doing. He came to enrich us spiritually and lift us from the moral poverty that we are afflicted with. We are all living in the dark and most of us have lost our way, so I suppose Guruji will show us the way, right?' 'Yes' was my only answer to every problem that people were facing the world over, from global recession to natural calamities to personal issues and relationships that seemed so fragile, and some even fractured. Divorce, for instance, has never been so rampant as it is today, particularly in a conservative country like India where the be all and end all of any Indian is saving up from the child's birth for that big fat Indian wedding, a crucial part of our culture. Parents' life mission is to get their children married as a moral and religious duty and once that's done, they let out a big fat sigh of relief! It is here that the wedding vows state not only till death do us part but till the next seven lifetimes together do us part! Nowadays, it's more like till divorce do us part or till the next person comes along to do us part!

On a serious note, divorce rolls off people's tongues more easily today than it did decades ago when the word was truly taboo. Irrespective of how severely damaging a marriage was, parents would insist that the miserable couple adjust to any length for the sake of saving face from society. Divorce was unthinkable but today, the financially secure woman has the option of walking out of a dreadful marriage thankfully owing to the rapidly changing mindset of the new affluent India. Divorce has become a healthy option to an unhealthy marriage.

One particular lady approached me with chronicles of her destructive marriage that she thought had no ending. After I spoke about Guruji's compassion and how He gives us strength to deal with our every ordeal until He can discard our karmic baggage, she felt liberated, as she knew then that one day she too would be free from her suffering. 'Closed doors are not necessary locked doors.' In Guruji's most humorous moments, He would state that a W-I-F-E is 'Worry Invited For Ever 'while a H-U-S-B-A-N-D is 'Horse Under Severe Burden And No Diversion!' My response to people's suffering was: 'Please visit the temple regularly as you would a physician if you had an ongoing medical issue and have faith as you would in your doctor who administers treatment. The results may or may not be immediate but if you look closely at yourselves, there would have been some inner changes that give you the strength to hold on for as long as you need to and the wisdom to know that you are in the right place.' After a point, the desires that we arrive with at the beginning may become futile and unimportant to us as our priorities and our perspectives make the shift. The journey of the soul takes flight as our material desires and aspirations take a back seat! What I realised over time is that I began to feel different from within and that reflected on how I viewed the world outside.

Over time, I felt a deep kinship with other disciples and I found myself longing to ease their pain by sharing my own blessings and the wisdom that came to me in the process. Although most people's intentions of coming to Guruji may be noble and pure, some of them fall by the wayside when they don't see instant gratifications. Hence, they lose their patience and quickly take a U-turn. Others persevere and although they arrive at the temple for the first time with aggrieved expressions, having lived lives that have possibly been trampled on, they are ready to give-it-a-try as Guruji used to say in His humorous moment: 'Here comes try-me and there goes not-for-me!'

I sat alone soaking in the aura of the inconceivably striking temple, pure and perfect whilst I prayed in earnest. I gently closed my eyes and with humility in my heart and possibly doubt in my mind, I implored Him to make my divorce official. I often had reservations about my own commitment to Guruji and my devotion was certainly nothing compared to the other devotees who sang devotional songs from their souls and served other devotees selflessly with love in their hearts. They adored Him without question and with positive surrender, they lived their tranquil and truthful lives. Meditation and spirituality can be most rewarding and being in a natural environment charged with divinity is both wondrous and wonderful.

The Good Lord knows I was nowhere close to being in the same space as them as they were all so well connected to Him. I had a tsunami in my mind and a hurricane in my heart! I was far from tranquil and I always wanted something and asked for it blatantly but then that was me, brazen. I would look Guruji in the eye and say what I had to unflinchingly. He would simply and serenely smile at me as if to say, 'What an idiot this disciple of mine is! Here she comes again with her thousand and one demands and her million and one doubts that question whether I will ever grant her all those pathetic demands! My poor pitiable child, maybe she'll get it someday. Until then I'll try and inject some sense into her!' Most people, He would state, salute the miracles and not Him and they would love Him only if He transformed their lives. Generally people never ask God for His light. Instead, they seek delight in the tiny, transient pleasures that soon wane or wither.

This time, He was not there in the physical form for me to offload my grievances on, so it was a challenge for me to believe that He was on course with me. I plead guilty for the initial stages after He discarded His physical garb. My mind entertained many doubts about His divinity but in due course, there were scores of positive changes in my life for me to pass them off as mere coincidences. Sometimes it's hard for ordinary minds like me to believe what we can no longer see but what was clear to spot was the sudden gusto with which my youngest brother, Sanjeev, began calling me to accompany him to the temple in the evenings every week for langar. His enthusiasm fuelled mine and this commonality strengthened our bond further. Before long, other cousins of mine, Hapu and Meenu, were also found there regularly and within months, most of my other cousins too along with my uncle and aunts! The icing on the cake was the social friends who too started appearing there and this common thread altered our equation to more than mere acquaintances. Guruji had left behind His Guru family for us to bond with and this gave us all a strong sense of belonging as well as a strong support system. This, too, Guruji had prophesied: 'There will come a day when your entire family will come to my durbar.

It was mission impossible when I embarked on my spiritual journey for me to convince my family to accompany me to Guruji. So I failed to see what was distinctly clear to Him. I doubted Him on this one too! As I have understood it and as Guruji used to state it, His ocean is infinite but He can give us only as much as our beliefs can accept. Our limiting beliefs are what hamper our spiritual growth and limit our blessings. It is far greater to sense Him than to see Him. Again the word 'surrender' springs to mind.

I grieved privately when He left unannounced but it did take me a few months before the reality of His absence sank in. I felt tears flooding my broken heart and wounded soul, a forlornness descending upon me like a cloud. I missed the intimate moments shared with Him, His humour, Him offering me tea and other sacred foods personally and the one-on-one chats. I felt the void of His physical absence and I was also afraid that He might have broken ties with me, leaving me unaided. He was gone or so I believed. 'Blessed is he who has not seen and yet believes,' goes a proverb. I had seen and yet I kind of disbelieved. I began to feel separated from the only life I knew after meeting Guruji. I missed His fleeting look of assurance that would state 'I am with you.' Pangs of longing filled me, as I felt displaced and uprooted.

I consumed the blessed food and tea, relishing every morsel whilst comfortably sitting unaccompanied on the lawn. I thought again as I observed some of the disciples sitting under the shade of the trees with eyes gently closed, meditating His name and smiling. They had never met Him and yet had hope in their despairing lives. Their suffering was far graver than mine and yet they believed. My! That's what you call surrender. Acknowledging the suffering of others minimises your own. I had so much more to be grateful for and their grievances always served as a reminder to me. I learnt that faith too is a gift. I inhaled the sanctified air deep into my lungs, then turning my eyes all around to make sure I wasn't being watched, I spoke out my thoughts: 'Guruji help me, please help me. I want to surrender to you but I just don't know how. I know you will do whatever is best for my soul but there is always a "but" and it is this "but" that keeps me from coming closer to you. Maybe you can take the darn thing away. I know you can as already you have accomplished most of the healing in me. Thanks and if you remotely feel that I'm worthy of your love, then please do the needful.' Then I sat in silence and quietly said once again 'Thank you,' the affirmation that became a central part of my existence.

My internal scenery, no doubt, was changing for the better each time I went to the temple. In addition, there was a deep realisation of the outer changes. What I understood from interacting with others is that we as people are not independent of each other as we learn from them, as they too are on similar journeys, and we teach them from our own. There is synergy between people and it is the collective consciousness that further empowers the temple. In addition, the concerted efforts of the disciples to look out for each other's welfare is what bonded us and gave us tremendous community spirit. The never-say-die support was unyielding and that is what kept the candle of our faith burning.

Each one of us has her/his own prescription to heal an emotional ailment but the one medication that worked without doubt was meditation. Though brief, those few sanctified moments spent in the temple cured me in relatively less time than it would have had I not been in that space. Of this, I am certain. Also it is the connection we make with the divine through regular evening visits for a couple of hours that enables us to overcome even the trivial everyday challenges that disturb our minds along with the ones that seem insurmountable.

When we are trapped in a situation under the lock and key of the same recurrent misery, it means that we are resisting grace from permeating our lives. When the Bible says, 'Let go and let God,' it means that accept your circumstances instead of fighting and on surrendering them to your God, you will be granted the karmic cleansing at the right time, space and sequence that you need, whether or not your 'What-the-heck-I-don't-believe-in this-crap' mind accepts it or not!

I had to bear the brunt of my previous karmic wrongdoings. Through them I had the good fortune of meeting my Master and allowing Him to cleanse my karma and elevate me to a higher level on not resisting but allowing Him to do His work whilst I did mine of being unreasonably restless!

On the 23rd December 2008, I was granted the divorce decree that put my mind to rest and changed me forever. So, it was really true that every story has an end but in life every ending is a new beginning.

12

The Inevitable Bumps on the Road

If we're always looking in the rear view mirror,
it's hard to keep our eyes on the road ahead.

Anonymous

The shoes that never fit and were never going to were finally discarded and my garb of pretence too dropped. I had the promise of a sugar-coated cake in my hands but did not know how to bite into it regardless of how delectable it looked. The initial euphoria of having made the grand exit soon turned into apprehension and angst.

A ton of bricks seemed to lay before me. The mortar, cement and every other building material were at my disposal. I was granted the blessings, the support and the love of my family, my daughters and the comfort of my friends but the prospect of doing it all alone was very intimidating indeed. I had all the resources without the know-how, so I sat clueless. I had no user's guide when I got married and I had no such manual after breaking it either. How would I rebuild my life and reconstruct a new self with new hopes, aspirations and a positive attitude that would be inherited by my then hurting daughters. I had to work laboriously to achieve my goal. I had to restructure a new belief system that would, without reservation, create an infallible self-image and self-esteem. It was a re-invention of the self and a re-discovery of a world with which I was previously unacquainted. That was a colossal task. I had to begin by instilling in me the self-worth that had dissipated over the years. I felt my energy dip at the thought of the mammoth assignment at hand!

I had read enough self-help books to know that my life rested in my own hands and the onus was on me to pick up the pieces and structure a meaningful and fulfilling existence with the protection and grace of my Guru. It was time for re-evaluation. Extensive reading enabled me to get the larger perspective. I needed to streamline my thoughts and head in the right direction. I had only myself to hold accountable for the choices I had made and the decisions I had taken that were to be life transforming. Regardless of the challenges that lay ahead, I had no regrets about leaving my past behind but I just didn't know how to get ahead.

I had frequent nightmares of individual bricks lying on the ground haphazardly and chaotically. I would sit amidst the heaviness of life, totally defeated. I would choke with tears in my throat but I would seldom release the tears for fear of my daughters sensing my weakness. I did not have the luxury of exhibiting my fragility and vulnerability, so I masked it not so well with a quarter brave face. The need of the hour was to be strong and sturdy in order to build a home of confidence, comfort, calmness and cheerfulness. I was the body and my children, the shadow. If I became inert and incapable, they would be the same. I felt responsible for their hurt and it was my responsibility to heal them and recreate a healthy happy home. They motivated me to surge forward. I was determined not to let society label my children as, 'kids from a broken home.'

It's the Indian woman thing again! You see, the Indian girl raised in a reasonably narrow-minded, orthodox family in the UK in the '70s where pleased Indians proudly held onto their Great Indian Values, did not entirely encourage a girl's economic independence. Hence, my financial insecurity. I had barely turned 16 when marriage proposals flooded our home like a tsunami. My only career choice was 'marriage' and for that, the only qualification required was the marriageable age of anytime after 19!

99.9 per cent of Indians have a thing for fair and lovely skin, to the extent that in India, parents urge their daughters to wash their faces with milk and apply yogurt masks to brighten their complexion. I didn't face that, thankfully. My parents were pretty proud of my complexion! However, even if I had a remotely ambitious streak in me to build a career, my father would gently manoeuvre me back by reminding me that I would soon be tying the knot with my knight in shining armour who would ride me away into the sunset. Well, the sun did set on me for sure and my own bright personality also got eclipsed awhile. I am convinced that the very reason why women choose to remain in self-deprecating marriages is for fear of being unable to support themselves financially. Hence, they bear it with a grin. Their homes are not broken but their spirits and their smiles certainly are. Most of them learn the art of keeping up appearances whilst the parents of these daughters continue to live in promise land. They refuse to allow the veil of illusion to lift as the truth is often inconvenient and it is easier to follow the herd.

It was a bitter pill to swallow but I was not earning an income to support myself. This part of my reality was pungent and hard for me to digest. Had the reverse been true, then that self-confidence would not have taken so long to rebuild.

Financial empowerment for a woman is as imperative as it is for a man but then in most Indian business families of that era, it was almost unacceptable for a woman to be bringing the bread home so to speak. 'Domesticity' was the only business that they were expected to be well versed at. Clearly, the only career choice I was given was 'marriage' in which I was expected to get a monthly allowance from my counterpart to successfully run the home.

After making my exit, there was complete financial support from my father and my brothers. Yet, I was plagued by a deep sense of insecurity and inadequacy. I went to pieces at the prospect of paying for all my expenses, the essentials and the luxuries. Every flow has its ebb, I suppose. I recall the first time my domestic help handed me the electricity bill after moving into my new apartment. I recall gazing at it for a few minutes before asking her what it was! For me, it was an alien object. Aghast, I opened it cautiously for it not to bite! I was bitten! 'So much?' was my astonished reaction only to learn later that 'Darling this is just the beginning of many more love letters that come through the post to break your tender little heart!' My heart bled every month for a few months until I became accustomed to the grief that the postman brought me. Then it became routine.

The life-after was, to begin with, a confluence of relief and grief but bills no longer disturbing me meant that I was progressing as I had larger issues to take care of. The only thing that I would get hot and bothered about was not paying in time. Wow! The eagerness to promptly pay bills!

The hurdles were overcome, one by one, and with each one crossed, I became more empowered, taking on a calm approach about mundane issues of paying bills! I had learnt to pace my life rather than race it! That's when I received a clean bill of confidence and I learnt that life is a complete D-I-Y (do-it-yourself) project and there are no one-size-fits-all solutions.

I also realised through it all that there is no exact 'how to', so I would need to take it step by step.

Guruji does our inner engineering in the subtlest manner and it is only through comparing, 'before and after' that I realise how much I have changed.

13

My Father

All the art of living lies in a fine mingling
of letting go and holding on.

Henry Ellis

In hindsight, the baggage of my past was still weighing me down.
I still lived in that place where I no longer was. Evoking memories
of the past meant not moving on and although there is no way of
easing the transition, I needed to acknowledge that I was out
of a very unhealthy situation and the ghosts of the past had to
exit my life. The only person who could pull me out was my
higher self that was witness to a troublesome marriage swaying
between between trepidation and trust. Trepidation seemed to be
the stronger partner and trust was cruelly overpowered. Trust is
needed to vanquish trepidation in order to live fully and fearlessly,
as it is the pre-requisite to a happy and healthy life too.

Trust is a very delicate thing and if it is not deeply instilled, it can very quickly shatter as I had also witnessed umpteen times at Guruji's divine abode with His disciples. A little knowledge is a dangerous thing and the less we understood about Guruji's truth, the more judgmental we were of Him. We 'all' did it; human nature. That is probably why He insisted on regular visits to the temple: to 'grow' we needed to 'go' to His ashram. The space was so charged with His energy that it healed me without my realising it. The space that we choose to be in does truly shapes us and we become that which we imbibe most. The devotees themselves, Guruji's extended family, were so full of compassion towards me. Each one was building me up whilst my own fears were tearing me down. The temple as well as the satsangs began spreading like wild fire in people's homes and I would attend them regularly as that gave me space to do some soul searching. What I realised was that I was coming in my own way, unable to let go of my overweight baggage and holding on to a very poor self-image that I projected most times. I wasn't fond of who I had become, hence the lack of self-respect. I was practically my own adversary who was weighing me down. I was going nowhere fast and I considered it necessary to wind down and create a space for myself. I needed to reveal all that I could no longer conceal. Healing meant letting my guard down and not being economical with my real feelings. It is at this point that I realised who was physically there for me and who wasn't. Love and friendship are both redefined; relationships are strengthened, weakened or broken. Once you recognise where the love and concern and pouring in from, you begin to cherish those very individuals, as they are the ones who walk you through your hardest times and hold you up when the chips are down. The rest is relatively easy.

On the 8th February 2009, six weeks after my official divorce, my father passed on after having been struck with cancer numerous times. He had fought a long-drawn battle with cancer with utmost dignity and a perpetual smile that lightened up the room as well as our hearts, inspiring us to meet our life's challenges too with the same invincible spirit. His entire life had been a message for others to live with utmost gusto and generosity, no matter what. He ensured that his life was inspiring to others whilst rendering them hope and strength. He was my strongest anchor. He left a huge vacuum in my life. As I had not been pre-warned about his imminent death and was absent from the last months of his life, I was grief-stricken and guilt-ridden. Even though death was looming over him and he was fast degenerating, I did not believe he would go as swiftly as he did. I missed him and after his departure, I began to retrieve everything he had given to me as a memento. I needed to reconnect with him on a spiritual level.

Through my search, I found a crumpled piece of paper with a handwritten couplet in Hindi on life and living. He had written it as I was leaving Manchester to return to Delhi after I had announced my decision to dissolve my marriage in 2006. It instilled in me immense hope and strength, particularly since it came from my father.

Knowing full well that he was wholeheartedly supporting my decision after witnessing decades of my struggle gave me the strength that I could not do without. He taught me to have the courage of my convictions and in the same breath cautioned me about the bumpy road ahead. Change such as this is never a picnic and I would be invited to many unpleasant situations where I would need to wear my garb of wisdom and good sense and hold above me the umbrella of divine protection. 'You will not sail through this and you will face a sea of troubles but you will certainly arrive at the shore much stronger and sturdier than you have been in a long time,' he said. 'The darkest night is that before dawn,' he reassured me. That is when he related his favourite couplet in Hindi, 'Dukh aata hai sukh dene ko. Man murakh kyo ghabrata hai? Jab zor ki garmi parti hai to badal mee barsata hai.' (Sorrow comes to give joy. Why then does the heart weep? When there is relentless heat the cloud bursts to shower rain.)

The most vitally important lesson I learnt from him was to live fearlessly and he would often express his disappointment in me whenever he sensed the fear that had taken over me over the years. He would state that he did not become successful through fear but through courage and calculated risk-taking. He too had made many mistakes but never looked back: 'Losers focus on what they are going through whilst winners focus on where they are going to.' He believed in me but also sensed a terrible lack of confidence and deep insecurity. I was no longer that chirpy, carefree and confident little girl of his. How time had transformed my entire mental and physical make-up. Long ago, during the early years of my struggle in the marriage, he once stated, 'Recognise what love is and what love is not.' This was in reference to my constantly defending my situation to save face and look good even when things evidently were not. Many women, in particular, keep a lid on bad marriages that seriously compromise their self-worth and dignity for fear of not making it on their own in the real world. It is always the fear of the unknown that keeps you in denial.

According to a Buddhist saying, 'Pain is inevitable but suffering is optional.' The most satisfying feeling in life is to make your own choices even if they are wrong. I assimilated all the wisdom I could draw from people, places and poetry for some understanding of my own circumstances. I sought counselling too although that was most random as I probably went twice to two different people! I was not prepared to give the councillor the 'laundry list' of my worries. I was determined to do my own cleaning through practical and pragmatic actions with the grace of my Guruji throughout. One of them heard me out and on the very first and last session, told me that I was a survivor! That did it for me. I knew I wouldn't go back but we became friends otherwise and her very talented daughter became my calligraphy and art student! C'est la vie!

After my father's demise, a major shift took place in my life. His death was a resounding wake-up call for me. I had been unable

99

to do him proud while he was alive and there was absolutely no way I would let him down after losing him. I urged him to smile at me from the other side of the visible but also to guide me to make me worthy of that smile! I desperately longed for him to be proud of me and I needed his guidance for that.

I recall standing before the altar of peace and speaking out my sentiments to him in private. My dialogue went something like this whilst holding his hand and gazing at his restful face: 'Dad, I'm so sorry I couldn't be there in the end to hold your hand and let you know how much I loved you.' I, like a million others I'm sure, always find it hard to utter those three priceless words to our loved ones while they are alive. I say it now a trillion times over for I never said it then even once.

'Also, Dad, I'm finding it very hard to do this alone without your support, so here I am asking for it again as I know for certain that you are stronger and happier on the other side, free of your physical suffering. I'm sure you are relieved to be released of this bodily pain.'

Tears rolled down my cheeks ceaselessly whilst I pleaded: 'Dad, please guide me and stay with me until I am able to walk again. I will always regret not being by your bedside when you breathed your last but you will live through me. Although I see you now and you see me too, I'm sure as you see things from a higher perspective and you can do and be more without the physical affliction. I love you. May God bless you with eternal peace and happiness.'

I choked on my tears as I left the altar and decided then that I would change my life. I did believe then as I do now that life is eternal and my father has only discarded his physical body. He is very much watching over his family. I was no longer vulnerable or sensitive and complacency certainly would be thrown out the window, as I would strategically go about making the changes. To be proactive was the order of the day and I would not only envision but also feel my father's guidance every step of the way. I had his

DNA. Hence, his 'Determined Never-say-die-Attitude.' Of us five siblings, I always felt like his weakest link but now it would be different. His radiant smile would shine on me and with a twinkle in his eye he would say, 'I knew you'd make it. I'm proud of you.'

I wondered deep down if my father had met Guruji on his journey up. It was just a thought, only a speculation, as I wouldn't get an answer to this one.

I took the flight back to Delhi with a heavy heart after spending three nights with my childhood friends in London. We had been absent from from each other's lives for 21 years, and they told me that I had changed for the worse! Oops! If that didn't confirm my need to change, then what would? They told me that my sense of fun and buoyancy had been pushed out of the door and my entire personality had become somewhat staid and sobre, void of spontaneity. Although my justification for my sobriety was my father's very recent demise, I knew in my heart that seriousness had practically become part of my make-up. My entire aura was different now with all my life experiences. The telltale signs of my ongoing anxiety were clearly read by my childhood friends who knew me like no other. Not nice! I needed to alienate the unhappy me. I needed to internalise the ancient truths about not judging even the bad experiences that had come my way, as they were ultimately a valuable part of my evolution as a soul. I had to shop for happiness and my first stop was, unsurprisingly, at Guruji's! I was lost before I first found Him. Then I was lost again as I had turned a different corner. Only He could take me safely back home to my real high-spirited self. The greatest victory would be the one I had yet to win over myself.

14

Cry Me a River

Success is not final, failure is not fatal.
It is the courage to continue that counts.

Winston Churchill

It was Sunday. I had been teaching art and calligraphy all morning in the privacy of my home to two young art students who marvelled at my work. I was born with the gift of fine handwriting that espoused the art of writing. Lending an expression to every experience and emotion was child's play for me, then dressing them in calligraphic letterforms was a walk in the park. I had a penchant for words and calligraphic letters came all too easily to me. I had hardly cultivated either, as God had been generous in His distribution of talents. Some highly talented art students came to me every week to learn various fonts coupled with embellishments and I was grateful for this as it afforded me unmeasured joy. After they left, however, I moved to my sofa and sat pensively.

Sunday afternoon and the girls along with my cousin Priya, who came to share my space a year after my separation, were out. I lit a candle before my Guruji's picture, which I did typically on a daily basis but this time it was not perfunctory. I placed the picture before me and I played a CD of soothing, soulful and sad Sufi tunes. Almost immediately, I realised how eclectic my taste in music had become, from my craze for the '80s tunes to the current ones to shabads and Sufi too. I closed my eyes and tuned myself to Guruji along with the melodies. I immersed myself in the moment and after a while, an ocean of tears ran down my face and I wept inconsolably, wallowing in self-pity! I was desperately trying to play the game of life as a single player, so I turned to Guruji for a casual chat: 'Guruji, I feel unsettled and that feeling appears to have become an integral part of me. I know that every flow has its ebb but I don't seem to be moving forward as I look and feel disconcerted. Introduce me to the self that was meant to be a pleasure knowing. Create a confidant, cheerful and certain me. I recognise through Your grace that the pursuit of happiness cannot bring me real joy but it is the search for myself that will lead me to it. Gently bring me back to myself without compelling me to go through hours, months and probably years of meditation programmes that promise catharsis. Kindly do not deprive me of my sleep as I cannot wake up before the crack of dawn to sit in silence amongst many others to realise the truth of my existence. Of course, this is the selfish streak in me that wants a quick fix but then I have undergone two decades of self-denial and rejection. I do apologise for continuously putting You under pressure to repair everything that I have broken with my own doing but then if not You, who will bring order into my chaos?

'Of course, today, I realise that my plea is so typically Indian in nature as I, along with millions of others, surrender to God, conveniently stating that I leave all my mess for You to clean up so that no effort is required from my end except to ardently pray. Even in that moment, there are a million and one fleeting thoughts that keep me from remaining focussed on my prayer. My end of the bargain is to believe in You and Yours is to believe that I'm worth it! Meditating in the real sense for hours, days and months on end means tons of discipline and restraint to get a glimpse of my karmic destiny and myself. I am such an external being who would do anything to keep me from taking a peek inside! Maybe I'm afraid of me. Maybe I'm afraid that I will never be the same again once I see the reality of who I am and what my true purpose is.'

I was not willing to summon up the necessary courage to do what must be done to unveil the noble truth. I had become comfortable wearing my old habits and familiar emotions that are at times tranquil and at times turbulent. The impermanence of everything from emotions to pain to love, to desire and to everything else can only be understood and transcended through serious meditation techniques. The experiential knowledge was truly imperative for me to realise how ephemeral even my current plight was but I chose the effortless way out as always, leaving every morsel of my life for Him to deal with so that I would not need to apply myself. Convenient! My unerring faith that my Guruji would miraculously disentangle all my knots prevailed. Of one truth I was certain—I had come all knotted up in desires to Him and He unknotted me to prepare me to climb higher.

I gazed into His eyes and I further asked Him if He heard me at all or if He even cared to and was willing to do more than what He had already done. I'm sure mine was the last voice He desired to hear! I also knew that I had to sense Him rather than see Him even though I had become so accustomed to His physical presence and found it hard to connect. I prayed for connectivity too! When would all my endless pleas end? I needed Him to redefine my path. For that, I pleaded with Him persistently. To draw strength from the higher consciousness sooner or later would enable me to regain the momentum of my life and move ahead with real happiness. With a quiver of anticipation and a pang of angst, I ended my prayer. I believed my distress would be quickly transformed.

The following morning, which was several months after my official divorce, I wrote affirmations. I read them repeatedly until they permeated my mind, then my life:

A   I am grateful for the love of my Guruji who tirelessly loves and protects me.

B   I have a healthy and happy relationship with my daughters.

C   My daughters Anishka and Sonakshi are truly happy, healthy and healed.

D   I am happy and emotionally healed.

E   I have abundance in my life.

F   I am grateful for the loving, caring and always-by-my-side friends in my life.

G   I am thankful for the sacred bond I have with my brothers and sisters-in-law who love me.

H   I am truly blessed to have love in my life.

I   I emit positive energy to all I meet.

J   I am an inspiration to other women.

K   I am truly grateful for the calligraphy students I have and for making a difference in their lives

L   I am earning a healthy income that affords me to fulfill all my whims and desires.

M   I am free from the shackles of my past negativity.

N   I am creating new possibilities all the time.

O   I am travelling frequently and extensively and educating myself through it.

P   My daughters are performing excellently in school.

Q   My daughters are able to get admission in top universities in the US.

R   I have love and respect in society.

S   I am a beacon of light for others.

T   I am a self-assured and self-sufficient individual.

U   I am truly happy from within and I radiate that emotion all the time.

V   I am an artist and a writer who inspires and makes so many people happy.

W   I feel truly attractive and loved.

X   My skin radiates sound health.

Y   My girls and I are protected at all times.

Z   My girls and I have an attitude of gratitude that draws in more positive energy into our lives.

Affirmations had become a way of life, as even to seek a smooth and easy divorce, I had affirmed it and envisioned the grand finale as a win-win situation for all involved. There were several other pages and pages of affirmations, and some not respectable enough to be put down in print!

It is both liberating and empowering to engender positive images. I learnt that in your personal visual landscapes, you can be and do anything. The more you visualise something, the more it is likely to happen. The small pictures too constitute the whole, so visualise both, the big and the small. Each of us has his/her own affirmations that get us through the day. What we think today takes us closer to where we would like to be tomorrow, is a result of those very affirmations. Just as thoughts carry energy, so do words. So what we speak, we become.

In addition, I made a daily gratitude list and slowly I began to think myself happier, healthier and in harmony with the elements around me. I set the bar much higher for myself. I was in tune with the events, all the while praying in earnest for victory that encompasses my former husband, my daughters and me. I also found a place in my heart to pray for his happiness and for him to realise that we could possibly be friends. After all, my fire and desire to get the divorce from him had been met. Now there was no reason to hold on to grudges. Above all, however, I prayed ceaselessly for my daughters' protection. I envisioned all that

I aspired for and more. My visual landscape became vivid and clear. I was climbing the mountain of faith on a daily basis and whenever I was burnt out, I visited Guruji's temple and my vitality would be replenished. The spiritual journey was arduous as I felt that the last shred of my karma had not yet been expiated, that I still needed to endure the struggle to learn a lesson or two more. Sometimes it takes an outside perspective to put your life in order.

15

The Pearls

Focus not on those who let you down
but on those who lift you.

Anonymous

God descends on earth to guide His loved ones in many forms.
Mine came in the guise of my friends and close family members.
They, too, were my friends: the pearls in my life's oyster. They
walked alongside during my most trying hour and as my journey
of vicissitudes continued, they kept my body and soul together.
I learnt through my divorce that the only currencies that are
never devalued are love and friendship, along with faith that was
experienced not from the periphery but rather from the epicentre
of my life. Since I was in quicksand struggling endlessly, it was
the firm hands of my friends that kept my head up so I wouldn't
drown. God could not be everywhere, so He made friends.

Clearly, in the early months of my separation, I was a disoriented soul who wore distraught emotions like an uncomfortably tight pair of jeans. Sadness is palpable and even my dog looked sad around me! I had to squeeze in a smile that was visibly out of place. I was consumed by the most daunting thoughts and this was obvious to most of my friends who could hear my head throbbing thunderously with turbulent thoughts! The past had moved out and its fragments also had to leave. 'Having a sharp memory is good but having the ability to forget is better,' councils Mary Jeanne.

I hadn't forgotten as yet and I was relieved that I didn't need to mask my real feelings and pretend to be anything other than what I was. Since I was not reticent either, mercifully I had my friends, my confidantes with whom I shared every molecule of my thoughts and feelings too, offloading my past grievances that would heal in time. Thank goodness for the mobile phone whose battery was forever low but which kept my spirits eternally high. Above all, thank God for my past that taught me well to appreciate every molecule of my present!

I particularly had and still have Rahul, my friend and soul mate who offered me the male perspective on my situation and walked me through setting up my life-after. He and I share a bond that cannot be labelled in conventional terms. I understand it to be a soul connection owing to his timely friendship, deep understanding, and empathy with my struggles then. There is a strong interconnection as he too seeks my guidance whenever the need arises although during the aftermath of my divorce, it was all about him nurturing me. He kept my feet firmly planted on the ground as I walked the unfamiliar path of being unaccompanied for the very first time in 18 years.

With his immutable and inspiring smile, he endured my then characteristic irritability too. His ability to lighten the load with his humour gave some comic relief to my days and in the moments when I was in form, there was a battle of wits as we employed our one-liners endlessly to amuse each other. Without a shadow of doubt, he turned the rough into smooth with his moment-to-moment inexhaustible support whilst enabling me to orchestrate a healthy and happy future for my daughters and myself. We had some pretty gruesome quarrels too that often got escalated. I would let off steam during my low tides and once the heat reached boiling point, we would slam the phone on each other. Then a few minutes later, we would make up! Either he'd apologise or I would and many years went by as our friendship went from strength to strength. Together, we found the way through the deep crevices to come out on the other side, stronger and sturdier.

My ongoing and growing concerns about this and that were diminished with his presence, as my attitude, priorities and values were all changing for the better. He dealt with every precarious situation with utmost concern. He unfailingly pointed at the silver lining each time I pointed at the cloud! I pointed at the pitfalls while he pointed at the stepping-stones! His endlessly patient ear and the subsequent counselling that effortlessly rolled off his tongue was a much-needed reassurance in my days that brightened with his genuine care and concern. Not once did he belittle my minute-to-minute queries or ridicule my unfounded insecurities, as he understood where I was coming from most of the time. He once quoted, 'Never, ever give up for that is the time that the tide will turn.' His belief in life, despite its tendency to punch us hard, enabled me to bounce back with refreshed vim and vigour. This kind of soul friendship comes with a life-long guarantee and it stands the test of time because its foundations are pure and pristine with no pretense. It falls in your lap as a consequence of blessings accumulated over several births.

Mr Optimism's dedication to my recovery gave me the might and muscle to overcome every hurdle and hardship on my road. When I believed that I was at the end of the rope, he tied the knot for me and taught me to hang on. He, along with my other soul-friends, steered me towards my new direction with a similar drive and dedication.

Anisha, my Guruji's sister who I was introduced to almost immediately after I met Guruji, was brought close to me by Guruji Himself. With the passage of time, we became inseparable and people at large began to get our names mixed up. That confusion originated from Guruji who called out my name when addressing Anisha and her name when calling out to me! We would visit the temple together regularly with our mistaken identities! Over time, we began to socialise with each other too as we realised that our pursuit for happiness was not confined merely to the temple, that there was a life outside it! When we weren't together, we were usually on the phone sharing every paragraph of our lives. We were convinced that we were Siamese twins except when she was at home with her husband. I am more than certain that the whole idea of remaining inseparable did pique the husband's curiosity leading his imagination astray but we spared him the ultimate gratification or perhaps the absolute grief!

On a serious note, Gautam, Anisha's husband, was a shoulder for me to lean on, as during my separation, he and Anisha would be at my doorstep every other evening to take me out either to the cinema, Costa or a cosy meal and a chat. We would visit Guruji's ashram together as they both understood that its aura gave me unmeasured solace. His keenness in bringing a smile to my then grim expression touched a chord in me. His gestures and his ongoing concern, as well as his most enduring patient ear, moved me.

I was an open book with unedited areas and that was acceptable at the time as it was my openness and honesty that drew people into my life with similar temperaments and on similar frequencies. If truth be told, all the chatting I did with my eternally patient friends, neighbours, some strangers and anyone who looked receptive enough to hear me out, is what contributed to my healing. I probably repeated all my grievances to all my friends and everyone else I knew and didn't know a million times over but not once did they give me a despairing look! My sadness was omnipresent and my poor daughters were as hopeless as I was but I believe they too had their support system that enabled them to deal with the situation. They were equally blessed with genuine friends and family that gave them emotional support.

The initial 3 months of my separation were the most traumatic, as I was not in the same space as my girls, living alone with sheer emptiness that moved in with me. It was during that time I received maximum support from Rahul on the phone from the crack of dawn, and Anisha and Gautam in person at dusk. Anisha and Gautam also sent me a delectable meal every lunch hour as an expression of their love for me for three continuous months. I will forget-it-not. They nurtured my heart, soul and body with divine love fresh from the heavens.

The promptness with which Rahul, Anisha and Gautam handled my life-after will go down in my memory book and will be safely guarded in the deepest vaults of my heart where all my priceless treasures are kept. Their after-care was totally hands-on; reconstructing my new home with unrelenting support and lifting the emotional cloud to allow the sunshine to brighten my home with a carefree gladness. Each kindled the dying flame of hope and the promise of a joy I had not known, with practical guidance. It was they who turned the dismal failure of events into a celebrated success. The everyday tedium and anxiety fell away, replaced by a barrel of gratitude as they each reminded me to maintain the high ground when struck with low and base thoughts and feelings. Rahul's perspective was, 'Put the past in a room in the basement, lock it and throw the key away,' whereas Anisha's take on the situation was spiritual, 'Unlock the door, clean it and let the light in.' True friends never get in your way unless you happen to be going down.

Some friends who were there during my marriage clearly chose not to be with me afterwards. Their disappearance was almost inevitable. There is expectedly a shift in the social scene as the dynamics of friendship change under such strain. It is human nature to begin taking sides, like in a match, shortly after two people separate and it was no different in my case as they quickly morphed into opponents, then very soon into aliens! They stopped acknowledging me as I too quickly reciprocated with a termination letter! What came to light is that those very friendships probably had paper-thin substance that could not have been sustained anyhow but then I positively chose not to dwell on those who let me down, cherishing instead those who held me up with sacred commitment. Some come into our lives as a blessing, some as a lesson, hence, for a season, but no one comes without reason. As luck would have it, the latter far exceeded the former, hence I had built more bridges than I had burnt. I had developed a well-meaning network of both supportive and stimulating friends. Don't worry about people in your past. There is a reason they didn't make it to your future.

Besides my inner circle of true, reliable friends, Anisha and Gautam, Rahul and Mamta, were Rahul, my lawyer, friend and guide, Seema, Shalini, Sumi, Shona, Shashi and Rati, Bonny, Bamby, Mini, Anju, Kenny and Kamal, Sabina and Renu, Shooshy, and scores of others (forgive me for not including your names but you do get to slap my wrist on meeting me!). There were my brothers, Rajan, Ajay, Sanjay and Sanjeev, their wives Rittu, Selena and Kajal. My cousin Priya came to live with me and became a great emotional anchor. Meenu, Ravi Hapu, Dimpyji and Guruji's sangat (blessed company) shared a strong sense of fraternity and were there for me unfailingly. I had earned unmeasured amount of credibility at the temple and they were only a phone call and a drive away. I felt indebted to my Beloved Guruji for giving me overflowing love with the sincerity and integrity that is impossible for any one individual to receive in a single lifetime. My cup was always spilling over with love and friendship and till date, I keep them all on a pedestal as sans them I would not have made the transition from abject hopelessness to absolute happiness. 'Don't walk behind me; I may not lead. Don't walk in front of me; I may not follow. Just walk beside me and be my friend,' had said Albert Camus

My former Buddhist members and friends had impacted me enormously as it was through faith that they enabled me to view the situation from the karmic perspective. When I saw it in that context, the blame game got over quickly and the bitterness dissolved in a hurry as compassion overrode the anger. I envisioned my former husband in my mind's eye and on seeing him, I forgave him and watched him exit the door of my life. I repeated this exercise until I genuinely did forgive and I felt light. Rakesh, the most articulate man I have yet to come across, was the leader of our chapter and his very able wife Kavita, lent me their patient ear throughout, following that up with sound advice on not just surviving post-divorce but thriving too.

Children inevitably suffer the emotional carnage of divorce, so it was all the more vital for me to restore all our lives to wholeness through the practice of faith. Ranu was another shoulder for me to lean on and her endearing laughter roared throughout my home on her every visit. Soon, however, my gaze turned evermore towards Guruji. I had to become absolute with Guruji as fragmented faith translates into fragmented blessings. Above all else, I naturally gravitated towards Guruji as my love for Him was profound and pure and I realised that nothing could substitute Him. He put both, my days and my devotion, into perspective and brought more smiles to my life to erase the tears. I only give a drop for the ocean I get.

My family's concern was unparalleled as my brothers came together to lend me their unrestrained financial and emotional support. My bonding, particularly with my youngest brother, Sanjeev, had become increasingly stronger and that thrilled me beyond words as his light-hearted nature drew a smile on my otherwise forlorn face. As our bonding strengthened, we began visiting Guruji's temple together. That was totally magical. It was incredibly elevating for me to observe him with his growing faith. Once a week he would call from work to ask me to meet him at the temple so that we could eat langar together. I never declined, as for me it was the ultimate pleasure and on leaving the temple, there would be an unspoken shared contentment on both our gleaming faces. We knew how close we had become on this sacred ground. Each time he bowed in reverence, I would discreetly pray to Guruji to shower His blessings on him. Guruji Himself acknowledged his purity and simplicity on meeting him for the very first time. He had urged me to get him along as often as possible but then at that point, my brother was not ready. I believe there is a time for everything. In my hour of despondency, his presence was invaluable to me. I had resided in his place for 3 months post-separation before I took refuge in my own space. Giving up his privacy to accommodate his sister was truly commendable on his part and I will forget-it-not.

The solace drawn from people who are there heart and soul for you when life seriously wears you out means so much more than you can ever quantify. It is like coming home to a homemade, hot vitamin-K (kindness) broth after being out in the densely dark, harsh cold winter's day. It nourishes your soul, refilling you with renewed energy and vitamin-F (fulfillment) after which you are simply consumed by vitamin G (gratitude) to be alive.

James Russell Lowell believed: 'All God's angels come to us disguised.'

Most of my angels came in the guise of family and friends. Fewer still came in the guise of my dates!

16

Dating

Life is a celebration of awakenings, of new beginnings,
and unexpected surprises that enlighten the soul..

Cielo

Being single again has its many upsides and one of the most
delightful ones is your eager-beaver friends being most
rapturous about introducing you to the other singletons at social
gatherings where the likelihood of meeting anyone unfamiliar is
next to naught!

I was clear at this point in my life about not being in search of
a life companion and I was determined not to fall in love, to spare
myself another matrimonial fiasco! Instead I signed up with my
trusted matchmaker friends to arrange non-committal, casual and
fun- filled dates preferably outside of our regular social circle. This
was the kind of stuff that my new dreams were made of!

I chose to go on casual dates to feel alive again and simply to feel again! No, I did not fall in love with all of my dates (barring a few!) and with some, there wasn't even a whiff of chemistry between us and others were simply a feast for the deprived eyes! Most were as short lived as a coffee and a chat, my all-time favourite pastime. With some who had the potential to be a friend, I went the extra mile of going for a meal that half way filled me with a scare that they might just misinterpret my gesture of friendship, so my energy would quickly shift gears and make me leave before we got to share a dessert! To most, my response was lukewarm and each one could not have been more different in tone. The overall experience was a healthy one as it was a sure sign of my recovery. I was enjoying being out with a guy without wanting to be the centre of his attention, his home, his miseries, his ambitions, his kitchen, his car, his TV room, his thoughts, his ailments, his holidays, his bedroom, his past, his PMT (permanent mental tension!), his office and his tax problems! I was healthily detached whilst having the wholesome experience of being indulged. Although I got off to a flying start, I slowed down immensely as my focus shifted from men to me! A paradigm shift!

It is not that my heart became impermeable but perhaps I exercised caution, as I believed it was not the right hour for commitment. Also my past that still needed healing, plagued my idea of a relationship. Hence, the few dates I had were experienced from the periphery rather than the epicentre. I had become heart-smart and opened up my heart for those who made it beat, The rest just beat it! The absolute truth is that initially I was losing my way, saying yes to every social invitation that came my way, which was probably in response to a sense of inner loneliness and having to face it had I been left alone, by myself! As a result, I also dated at random, not screening my suitors I deemed interesting, well enough. Playing the dating game, though, kept me motivated as the extra weight that had recently found a loving home on my mid-riff also came off! As plenty of men and women know, unhappiness can very quickly turn into fat, so dating kept the pounds off! If and when I did find myself to be falling in love due to my vulnerability, I quickly recognised that once again, I was getting trapped in a potentially unhealthy situation. My purpose of dating was to uplift my spirits and my morale. In the bargain I made well-meaning male friendships that by far carried more weight than anything else. I met them with no idealised visions of orderly evenings in my head, so each of them turned out characteristically interesting! Till date, one of them is my friend and we meet for the occasional coffee date and a laugh about how either one of us could have fallen in love with the other to destroy the other's life!

A seasoned guy with an evolved thinking, he had been married and divorced and had taken a pragmatic view of recovery. He empathised with me the day we met and beguiling as he was, he invited me out every other day for the first ten months of my separation. I juggled between Anisha, Gautam and him. We ventured out to places I had never seen in all the years that I had lived here, in Delhi. We ate, drank and danced. In short, he introduced me to the happy pill and his sense of adventure added a spark to our dates. He quickly became the wind beneath my broken wings as he had an arresting sense of humour to match his captivating looks. His bright and breezy personality lightened my load making our dates healing and therapeutic. In fact, he ticked all the right boxes and he certainly knew how to get me out of my box. He also had volumes of advice to lend on post-separation trauma as he was balanced in both—his head and heart. It was clear that the ugliness of it all had shaken me to the core that caused me to doubt and mistrust but he reassured me that by following my instincts, I had a better chance of finding happiness some day. He spoke from a place of personal experience and after listening to him,

I had a clear perception of my past and became determined about not allowing my unfortunate experiences to taint my view on relationships. So why didn't I fall for him? I did! However, right from the word 'go', we decided to keep it platonic in view of my wrong timing. I was obligated to hold myself back! No, seriously at this point in my life, I was not necessarily an optimist as far as romantic love was concerned. Today, we remain close friends and he is now married a second time round. I sure missed the bus! The few others I dated were singing a different tune to me, so I bid my farewell in a hurry! I haven't seen them since and they need not go down in my memoirs!

The experience of dating was not always a fine one but it was cathartic in the larger scheme of things. Although it was inviting and threatening in the same breath, there was always something to learn about myself through each one of them. Deepak Chopra has said, 'However good or bad you feel about your relationship, the person you are with at this moment is the "right" person, because he or she is the mirror of who you are inside.' We see our own reflection in others. We get a glimpse of the self in the person that we are with. Hence, we get closer to knowing ourselves!

My emotional health certainly perked up as I became increasingly centred, calm and comfortable in my skin. In addition, it confirmed my need to develop a voracious appetite for something more palatable—painting! I had the liberty of choosing my own palette here without worrying about whether I was wearing the right colours or not. I had the flexibility to create my own canvas without compromise. Karma and circumstances do create a canvas but the real painting is done through free will.

Collectively, Anisha, Seema and Rahul along with my other two closest of friends, Bonny and Sumi, decided that I ought to paint by day and party by night and so it was. My fate was sealed! I decided to paint and paint till my floors would be painted red and I would party and party without painting the city red! In other words, the latter did not stimulate my senses anymore so I focussed on the former without question. When you decide to take on only a few meaningful activities in a day with utmost sincerity and dedication, they breathe and take on a new life and, in time, they present a broad window of opportunity.

17

Art Classes

Difficulties mastered are opportunities won.

Winston Churchill

Finding your true vocation in life is like finding your true love. It can be a lifelong romance unlikely to cause you any heartache and it protects you even when the forecast is dismal! It is positively elevating and profoundly satisfying.

My longing to be an artist was overwhelming. The talent was apparent but I needed a compass. The need for finding a mentor was not realised by me alone.

In early April 2009, Rahul gave me my customary morning call to check on me. After I shared my plight of not knowing where to look for a mentor, he promptly urged me to call up renowned artist Kanchan Chander, who was also a teacher and a close friend of his relative's. I rang up and asked if I could register myself for her classes. She invited me over before enrolling me to get a sense of my work and my objective for learning, as most of her students were preparing for universities abroad like Parsons in New York and London School of Art, St Martin's and other eminent universities overseas. I simply wanted to paint without any lofty goals in mind.

On meeting her, we instantly became friends and she opened up her portfolio, her studio and her fridge! Chilled beer is what she motioned me to pull out while she had the bottle-opener in her hand instead of a paintbrush! 'It's too hot for tea or coffee,' she reasoned. 'Beer is cooling, especially on a scorching hot day such as this.' An intoxicating way to begin I thought! Her effervescent personality uplifted me already.

'Of course!' I agreed. She was after all my potential teacher and I wasn't going to take a rain check, so she poured beer after beer into my glass whilst I poured my heart out hour after hour about my earth shattering experiences in India during my marriage and my build-up thereafter! I unbolted my past whilst she unlocked hers only to discover that we were both divorced! I was an aspiring artist while she was already an accomplished one. We both spoke on love, life and divorce for hours as we drank satisfactorily for hours! I did very well considering I was a teetotaller! Bravo Anita!

I left with a broad smile and a song in my heart. I waved at her vigorously as you would if you were out of control! I got into my car and emphasised that we would meet shortly for me to learn to paint and not to drink, as I was clearly lousy at that.

I started immediately after getting hold of my materials and gaining sobriety! My first class was all about perusing through her artwork in print and viewing her many canvases that she had prepared for her forthcoming exhibition in Brussels. She had exhibited the world over many times and had received much recognition for her work. I was sufficiently impressed and inspired. After viewing my work she simply asked me to be regular and dedicated, as she was there to train students for a higher level.

Thankfully she saw promise in my work and believed that I merely needed fine-tuning my style. I set the wheels in motion by not only attending the school three times a week but painting ardently in my studio at home. Almost every waking hour was spent trying out different textures, tones and forms. Simple, elementary exercises like mixing colour and trying my hand out at creating different patterns and designs for the backdrop became routine. I felt positive about learning, as I saw changes in my work and in my attitude towards it, as well as a shift in attitude towards myself.

I was on my journey and my genre had clearly become Lord Ganesha, the Hindu Elephant God who is the Remover of Obstacles. God knows who chose who? How appropriate!

I had embarked on designing Lord Ganesha practically immediately after I moved into my new apartment post-separation. I would sit idly with a sketch book on my lap and the images I drew were incredible semi abstract designs of Lord Ganesha, though all on paper, as I didn't have the heart to ruin a canvas! For me, the idea of painting on canvas was daunting as I had always been a pen-on-paper artist whose expertise lay in calligraphic letterforms designed within. Encompassing Ganeshas and, before long, 'Oms' and Buddhas also became an integral part of my designs. This exercise afforded me time to think, reflect and introspect, to realise my own capacity.

A few months after joining Kanchan, the artist, she booked me for a group show with three other upcoming artists. This placed me on the hot spot and I recognised that I needed more training than I was receiving. The pressure motivated me to work tirelessly from dawn to dusk, putting me in a positive frame of mind. I felt a deep sense of purpose. From the comfort-zone, I was moving into the grow-zone. Slowly I was breaking old habits of hiding behind my past as an excuse not to move ahead. I was moving in a new direction, developing more positive, can-do attitudes that banished those counterproductive states of mind and unhelpful habits that I had a tendency towards, and that hindered my progress. My receptivity to learn increased my productivity and although I was tense about the show, there was a wave of excitement too that I could hardly contain. 'I can is more important than your IQ.' Robin S Sharma was spot on!

Most importantly this daily exercise allowed me to let go, spending the entire day without seeing anyone or chatting endlessly on the mobile with more than a couple of friends in a day. Now I was comfortable in my skin. Alone meant all-one, a sense of completeness filled me. I could feel Guruji pulling me out of the realm of fear and slowly but surely, moving me into the realm of faith. I now know for certain that meeting Kanchan and breaking my fears of the canvas is one of the many great experiences that I drew into my life.

My friends generously expressed their belief in my work rekindling the dying flame of creativity in me. By believing in me, they opened up new vistas for inner expansion. Kanchan, too, was a great mentor who believed in my work and encouraged me ceaselessly over a glass of beer, which I enjoyed sharing with her whilst I would seriously talk till the cows came home! I believed I was creatively shattered but that was clearly far from the truth. I was not seeking celebrated success but that which would revive my self-belief. I longed for a positive response to our show. Meanwhile, there was a larger and more important task at hand that needed careful handling emotionally and rationally.

18

Anishka

Looking and moving higher.

Anonymous

My daughter, Anishka, gained admission in one of the world's leading private universities in the heart of Los Angeles. I was dealing with all my unfounded fears one by one and the next one was to settle Anishka down in USC in LA in August 2009. I hadn't travelled more than a continent away post-divorce and now I was challenging myself once again with a heavy heart. Travelling and parting ways with my baby who I felt I had neglected in the past few years during my own emotional recovery, was a grave challenge staring me in the face.

I questioned the years gone by so rapidly, particularly the recent ones in which I was predominantly busy in mending my broken life. I was resentful towards time and my mismanagement of it, as I felt I had largely missed the recent years with my girls. I would turn back the clock and do it differently in a heartbeat. By being more balanced and level-headed, I would protect them from the inevitable post-divorce traumas and whisper to them every night that life will get better in spite of it all. There are no second chances and I could not undo what had been done. The only way to go is forward and our future is not stamped by our past.

I said a little prayer in my heart to the two strongest men in my life. Dad I'm going to settle my baby there in LA, so please accompany me.

'Guruji, enable me to conquer my last shred of fear, and to let go of the last morsel of the past that immobilises me. Let me break free from the self-created trappings and spread my wings in the same manner that Anishka is about to. Kindly take her under Your divine wing, as I know You will. Give her strength and wisdom to always soar high in the skies that lead to her and others' happiness. In the silence of my soul, I always say, 'Thank You' as I always say, 'I Love You.'

At this point in my life, I had engaged myself in the practice of involving Guruji in some of my activities. I was sometimes able to feel His presence in my endeavours and engagements. 'Feel me in your heart as that is my favourite dwelling place,' He had said to me a while back.

Soon, Anishka and I were on a smooth flight to Los Angeles with turbulence in my heart. She was about to leave a void in my life but she was filling hers with the extraordinary prospect of finding herself. Education is by far the greatest asset and she chose her path well, hopefully to build it with a sound career too. I felt tears of pride and sadness sting my eyes as I glanced at my sleeping beauty on her seat. How life passes us by. She was 18, blessed with the best of beauty and brains and I was blessed to have both in both my daughters! I remember distinctly being 18 and my father hosting the most rocking party for me with black and white as its theme and both guys and girls to celebrate the never-forgotten occasion where guys danced in one corner and girls in another! I had the prospects of a marriage hanging over my head whilst, today, Anishka has a bright forecast with a pragmatic attitude and approach to life that yet supports her Indian values of building a healthy and happy home someday. People and their attitudes have changed enormously towards women and their progress. The women of today have a drive that does not park their lives in domesticity and gives them the option of shifting gears from home chores to the corporate world and more.

As Anishka slept blissfully, I prayed to Guruji for her resilience. It is not how severely life knocks us down but how well we bounce back and my concern was that she mustn't allow the knocks to shatter her self-confidence and self-esteem. I wanted her to come out on the other side knowing that she had conquered the most difficult times to make the very fibres of her being mightier and more magnanimous. If we come out of a belittling situation, we can stand taller than anyone else, knowing that we have fought our battles and won. Winning is an attitude and I always wanted her to wear that attitude like a precious piece of jewellery to accessorise her personality.

I couldn't help but dwell on the thought that change really is constant, that in the fleeting nature of events, what also must remain constant is our inner equanimity to enable us to cope with the outer changes. Charles Darwin says, 'It is not the strongest of the species that survive, not the most intelligent either but the most responsive to change.'

On successfully settling her in on the incredibly impressive campus of USC and praying in earnest for her happiness in my heart, I made my way to Orange County to stay with a doctor friend, Sue, for a few nights where she had the most pleasurable surprise in store. On the following morning of being with her, she motioned me to her car and showed me the driver's seat. 'You're driving!' She commanded!

Where we were going was the second surprise after the first shock of me in the driver's seat on a highway on foreign soil where I had never driven before! I was conquering my fears by confronting them and Sue was successfully enabling me to do just that. 'Keep driving!' was all I was getting every 20 minutes or so until a whole hour passed by with me confidently driving on the right-hand side of the road as opposed to the left in England and on any-and-all-sides-of-the-road in Delhi! I was flying by now and sooner than I imagined, we were parked in Mexico! Good gracious!

After spending half a day there with Sue administering medication to the underprivileged, we drove, I mean I drove, to San Diego, to La Jolla. Now that was a breathtaking surprise along with the surprise of me having overcome the fear of driving on foreign land. When we are pushed into the deep end, we can either sink or swim.

We arrived at the most stunning sceneries on earth. The sounds of the waves flowed through me, making me one with nature. The 'I' in me dissolved and I melted in the moment. Nothing mattered, the past or the future. I was floating and it was this sensation I wanted to hold on to, not realising that this too shall pass. It is the ephemeral nature of things that needs to be understood, that allows the detachment to happen. Watch pain and pleasure as though it were one and neither is here to stay. Standing on the edge of the aqua-blue Pacific was the most extraordinary experience of my life and its vastness made me realise how diminutive my issues were. The trivialities of everyday existence are what need to be transcended to get a glimpse of the larger picture. I let go of everything allowing the spectacular Pacific Ocean to wash away all my fears and my memories of the past. Gone. As for the future, the best thing is that it comes one day at a time.

The lesson of forgiveness is the hardest, and that till date it is not absolute. Is it ever? Forgiveness comes in minute proportions depending largely on the place I'm in. If I'm having a good day, I send out divine light and healing to my former husband but on a rainy day, I feel differently and the light and healing turns into darkness! No, I'm not Mother Teresa and arriving at that noble place will take me lifetimes, or so I currently believe. Who knows? Yet, I still prefer to forgive him in the here and now! One of my umpteenth pleas to God is that He should give me a hand in letting go of the past experiences with my former husband. After all, who doesn't want to travel light?!

I did feel lighter, much lighter after visiting California. Something shifted. Closure did come when I left it to 'time' to take care of it and I somehow found it in my heart to forgive. Blaise Pascal reminds us: 'Time heals griefs and quarrels, for we change and are no longer the same person.'

Travel put things into perspective and I realised that I too am merely a traveller on this journey of life. From this moment on, I was going to drive through every road with the aim of not cutting corners but going around them with absolute awareness of the inevitable bumps. Each bend is not an end but the beginning of another road. The utmost lesson for me was to drive fearlessly, boldly and bravely. I no longer over-estimate the power of fear, as I know that it can be overcome with the power of faith and the inner fortitude that it brings. Fear is toxic and, as I stated earlier, I needed to take a step back and not look at it subjectively as if I were an integral part of it. Instead of seeing fear as the ultimate obstacle, it needs to be seen as a challenge, to be overcome. I triumphed over my each fear, one by one, and then I realised that they were all unfounded. The outcome I feared of each of my action, especially the one after leaving my husband and my inability to survive in the world, was unsubstantiated. That was indeed my deepest fear, of not being able to rise after the fall, but time proved me wrong. Time reveals our true character as it ripens all things.

I could've stood for hours on the brink of the Pacific in quiet and deep contemplation as, at that moment, I felt heaven and earth become one. The tranquillity of the water permeated me and I knew then that a higher force had healed my past and was taking care of my future too. I bowed before the ocean and said audibly, 'Thank You Guruji.' I became emotional, dreamy, poetic and peaceful as I embraced beginnings and endings. I savoured the scene for several more minutes before I turned back but before leaving, I whispered yet another desire, 'Let my art be recognised.'

As the sun set on the tranquil Pacific, Sue and I dined in a restaurant just on its fringe from where the view was transcendental. We watched the sky turn from orange to crimson, then yellow, as we spoke about life and its celebrations, this being one of them. The beauty of the moment was clearly captured in my memory. The other memory that came alive here was of my father's whose heart was, without doubt, beating amongst us. We dined and discussed love, life and what a dreadful divorce she, Sue, was going through. Then the sky turned ebony. The sun had set and we drove home to rest.

On arriving in Manchester after LA, I planned to imbibe the sights and sounds of Central London and so it was for three nights with my cousin Hapu, and her daughter Aatika who was visiting England from Delhi. I met my friends Rahul and Mamta too for dinner at Buddha Bar, which was truly amazing. Mamta's father treated all of us, including Hapu and Aatika, to an unforgettable meal in the most surreal ambience.

The following days, we travelled to all the tourist places with me guiding them, day in and day out, before I exhausted myself pleasurably and then decided to return home to Delhi. Three days later, I landed in Bangkok with Sonakshi for a mother-and-daughter bonding over a long weekend! It was as lovely as it was liberating as I booked myself in the Four Seasons in Erawan. It was during our stay that I was inspired to write this book! Every time I hit the sack, I would get inspired to pen down a few words and so I did. During the days, I went for massages whilst Sonakshi shopped satisfactorily knowing that her mother was nurturing her. After the shopping spree, we would dine at the exquisite area of Erawan in various hotels. Her joy is etched in my mind and by now I was flying!

19

The Art Show

Dreams are renewable.
No matter what our age or condition,
there are still untapped possibilities within us
and new beauty waiting to be born.

Dale E Turner

One of my homemade recipes for recovery and self-discovery
post-divorce was to challenge myself in areas where I felt weak.
I honestly believed that my art was not up to the mark but I was
more than prepared to give it my all. I had learnt the art of seeing
my success in my mind's eye. I worked conscientiously until I
oozed confidence. On returning from Bangkok, I grounded
myself once again, working diligently till the show.

I was forever grateful for the deep, steady and supportive
friends who enabled me to paint single-mindedly. Rahul would
call regularly to check what was in my hand—my paintbrush

or my mobile! My friends knew my weaknesses as well as my strengths. The beauty of all my friendships was that they had all seen me and been with me at my worst and now they smiled with me sharing my laughter at my best. Elbert Hubbard rightly said, 'A friend is one who knows you and still loves you.' I related to them differently by this time as my inner canvas had changed. The non-essential baggage had been discarded and now I was focussing on the essential.

Seema, my beloved friend and agony aunt, managed to get me admission in one of Delhi's most prestigious art colleges towards the end of September 2009 after I returned from Bangkok. That was the turning point as I learned oil on canvas three times a week in a very disciplined environment that wasn't mediocrity friendly! Painting in a strictly professional environment enabled me to work diligently without distractions and deviations. Most importantly, it enabled me to overcome my fright over ruining a canvas! Painting without inhibitions was the most effective prescription for emotional health too and I was able to develop a broad spectrum of themes widening my limited vision. Amongst the students, there were those who were already professional, and their dedication further motivated me, and others who were deeply immersed in their work striving to reach their goals. It gave me immense pleasure to see the treasures of creativity, talent and strength in each of the students with their own unique style, each committed to their vision. I believe talent lies in each one of us but it needs to be unbolted and set free by clearing away the impurities of fear and self-doubt from the depths of our souls. What we believe in is what shapes our world.

Seema, Rahul, Anisha, Sumi and Bonny were shaping my world by keeping a close watch on me to ensure that I was not deviating from my route! I would receive a message from Seema saying, 'Seeing you there, babe!' every time I made a commitment, so even if I desired to quietly slip away from the commitment, I was gently pushed back on track. Her mantra was, 'Babes, never give up!' Rahul, on the other hand, would call in the morning and firmly remind me of my class and my debut exhibition. He did not allow me to lose sight of my goal and reinforced my belief by commending me on my mediocre works too! On days that I was not so driven and inertia took over, my most enduring friends made sure that I did not get side-tracked. I was profoundly grateful to be observed at such close proximity, as I knew I needed to be kept on a tight leash to get back on track. The vibes I gave out then were probably stating, 'Please hold my hand, as without you, I will lose my way.' Their TLC (tender loving care) and PLC (patient listening capacity) will go down in my memory book and my recipe book! Their homemade recipes for eating happy pies everyday was part of the recovery given by each of them.

I had merely 5 months to showcase my work in one of the top galleries of Delhi. Although my desire was not to receive resounding success, it was one that would restore my self-confidence. I was under close scrutiny and with my most intimate friends to broaden my aesthetic vision, my goal was just around the corner.

After painting stroke by stroke, day in and day out, until D-day, I visited Guruji's temple once again to seek His blessings. I entered it knowing full well that He would lend me sufficient support for my debut show. I bowed before His photo and smiled before I spoke. 'Here I am asking You for a piece of good fortune once again for the untold time! All I do is ask for every task! My demands are infinite but this one means a lot. Thank You!' I never forget to thank Him. Never.

On the nail-biting eve of the show, Gautam and Rahul assisted me in displaying my work to afford it aesthetic appeal. It took practically all evening and I could feel butterflies flutter in my empty stomach whilst the two good men dutifully placed the artwork with their might and muscle. Meanwhile, I lost my appetite and were is not for the continued reassurance from my friends on the phone and these two wonderfully supportive friends displaying the exhibits, I would have lost my nerves too!

My finest hour arrived on 1st April 2010, also Sanjeev's birthday, and my first and most encouraging viewer was my brother, Ajay and his wife, Selena. I had gone home to change my attire and they reached the exhibition before me. After viewing my work, they called to congratulate me on the surprisingly striking work. The pride in their voices was enough to make me ecstatic and I could not stop laughing and thanking Guruji for His blessings. Thereafter, my other brothers Sanjay from the UK and Sanjeev, my youngest came and lent me enormous support. Sanjay, too, was shell-shocked and stated that he wasn't even aware of this hidden talent of mine. The pride in his eyes was a clear reflection of my father's and I knew he was present.

Besides my closest friends, particularly Seema who stayed till the end, there was a flood of people pouring in. To inaugurate the show, Kanchan and I had invited the eminent photo-journalist Mr Raghu Rai, also Guruji's staunch disciple. He graced the occasion and before leaving, placed his hand, on my head blessing me and wishing me every bit of success. I was every bit moved. It was my finest hour and I had never been more contented. Anishka had wished me from her university in LA and Sonakshi, my younger one came with my relatives to stand beside me. My former in-laws also graced the show. It was surreal as the media continued clicking photos of my works along with the works of the other three artists, and my mentor Kanchan Chander. It was great teamwork. I was in seventh heaven as I felt the gods smile down at me along with my father. 'I knew you would do it. I am proud of you,' my father seemed to be saying.

This incredibly pleasing experience put everything into perspective. I had so many things to be grateful for: my personal and now professional equations, my talent and the love all around me that knew no bounds. My past, present and future, all became one and I viewed my life solely from a positive angle. My soul bowed before Guruji and once again whispered a heartfelt 'Thank You.'

Following the show, my brothers invited me for a double celebration—Sanjeev's birthday and my success story—to one of the most prominent restaurants in Delhi. As the wine poured into their glasses, they inundated me with a ceaseless flow of compliments. My soul was laughing and I was continuously thanking my Guruji, my father, my mother, my brothers, my daughters, my extended family including my former in-laws, my friends, my teachers, the birds, the flowers, the skies, the universe and all the positive elements in and around it. I had turned the corner that I had envisioned.

That night, I was born again and there was only one way to go—ahead. Success is never attained single-handedly and I was vividly aware of the concerted effort of those who deeply and sincerely cared, handling the nuts and bolts of my new life and setting the tone for happiness. This ignited in me an eternal love for mankind and an everlasting trust in the divine. Guruji had once stated, 'I have come to restore faith in people and to remind them that there is God. In this world where mankind is on the verge of moral bankruptcy, I have come to enrich you spiritually and to realign your morals and values.'

I felt enriched by the mere thought that I was blessed and that was clear to see by the people and situations that I was constantly drawing into my life. My past was quickly withdrawing itself to give room to the present that was shaping my future.

20

The Travel Bug

*Happiness is not a station you arrive at
but a manner of travelling.*

Margaret Lee Runbeck

I recall making my New Year's resolutions at the beginning of 2010—to travel as frequently as I could throughout the year and I did just that. We practically write our own stories. If I convince myself that something is going to happen, then it usually does. On that creepy note, I ensure that I wish for the right thing that doesn't make me fall flat on my face!

In the first six months of 2010, I travelled firstly to Goa to stay with Bonny in her holiday home. This was in February before the show in April and there we planned to travel to Athens and Prague post-show but waited until May after the volcano Eyjafjallajökull in Iceland stopped erupting. Not abandoning our plans meant strengthening our friendship in one of the prettiest cities I have ever come across. Athens was not a patch on Prague as far as its unique architecture and culture is concerned but both cities combined made it a dream.

In the next leg of my travels, Anishka, Sonakshi and I flew to Istanbul in June for a vacation that will remain etched in my mind. Both my sweethearts were pleasantly surprised by my sense of adventure as I booked us every tour possible in the three days of us being there to cover every spice market, mosque, bridges including the renowned Bosphorus and all else that was worth a visit. My girls witnessed a sea change in me and this really bridged the emotional gap between us as we chatted ceaselessly about the times gone by as well as those to come. I had clearly changed inwardly and outwardly, as I was no longer projecting my worries or fears but rather a joy and freedom I had never felt before. The entire experience was truly empowering for me as I had completely overcome my financial insecurities by then and with ease I booked our first vacation with all three of us together. The sky, really, was the limit! My spirits were soaring high as I was living my life with heightened awareness and joy. Guruji really had injected in me an unmistakable zeal for life and love. As I began to savour the flavour of life, I felt truly animated. My rebirthing meant a renewal of mind, body and spirit. Once I took the step of believing in myself, then happiness was mine to embrace. I took a leap in what seemed dark only to emerge into light. How liberating and self-empowering it is to find yourself by triumphing over your every identifiable fear. Only those who have conquered them, proactively, can understand this. The satisfaction of confronting and then conquering the fears is immense.

In a sense, destruction is good as it enabled me to grow again and allow myself to open up to the universe's secrets that brought vitality and vivacity to my existence. Destruction has the power to break us and has an equal power to kindle the fury in us to rise after the fall. HG Wells summed it up well: 'If you fell yesterday, stand up today.'

To step out of the shadows into sunlight meant reinventing myself as well as my attitude towards life. I learnt to live in the moment to truly savour its meaning. In brief, I learnt to live again like I hadn't before, noticing the minutest details of my surroundings such as the shades of leaves on the trees to their varying barks to the distinct patterns in the open skies to people who walked beneath them. I realised how much my mind and my vision had closed up. That is what happens in our moments, months and years of despondency. The breadth of despair was there to engulf me but something higher and greater than myself had rescued me. Recognising prolonged dejection is the first step in bringing about internal change that reflects the external. Leo F Buscaglia reminds us: 'Risks must be taken, as the greatest hazard in life is to risk nothing.'

The last word on maltreatment in a marriage is 'self-empowerment.' Whether you work on your inner fortitude during a bad marriage or post-separation, the road to happiness can only be travelled on once the vision is clear and you dispel the clouds of fear. Happiness then starts from me, my inner life and then travels out. I believe it vital at this point of my writing, for me to state that self-empowerment cannot be achieved alone. It comes with community support, spirituality that is both practical and theoretical through extensive reading and understanding that gives you a sense of where you came from and why, where you are going and how. The practical spiritual support I received from my Guruji, however, was unparalleled. What He gave me cannot possibly be measured in words. When one door of my life closed, all others remained shut too! It was the heavenly door of my Guruji's heart that flung itself wide open for me to walk through only to find that by doing so, all other shut doors opened too.

of infinite creativity and connectivity. Once I had empowered myself through self-search and the eternal blessings of my Guruji, I was able to see things for what they were. The veil of ignorance lifted and the manipulations surfaced and realised. My goal was

139

happiness post-separation and my internal mantra was 'love.' I made room for selfless love and a non-judgmental approach to people and relationships. Even though I was desperately sensitive to their view of me then, I was surer of my own view of myself that allowed me to be comfortable in my own skin. I always pray for people who don't quite grasp the meaning of ugly domestic situations. They look at you with raised eyebrows but then not everyone can grasp a subject so sensitive in nature. I have learnt to log into 'Let it be.com' and 'let them be.com!'

Through the myriad changes within a short span of time, from my divorce to settling myself and the girls down, to our new apartment, to taking my cousin, Priya, from England under my wing, to the demise of my father, to Anishka spreading her wings and flying to LA after a few years, I felt a growing sense of inner poise. My external composure now began to correspond with my internal climate. Equanimity of the mind and spirit was attained and now there were yet a few more dramatic changes in the pipeline, so once again I would turn to my divine engineer to get His tools out to loosen that which no longer mattered and to tighten that which did. He knew best and I was fast learning not to interfere in His plans.

Guruji, the Engineer of my internal mechanism and the Architect of my outer world was also the divine navigator who was about to steer me in a totally inconceivable direction. With His divine compass He was about to show me a direction that would set my life in stone.

21

Turning the Page

*I had figured out my cast
and now I needed to figure out my life's plot.*

Author

Following our vacation in Istanbul in the month of June, we attended my brother Sanjay's 40th grand birthday celebrations in Manchester along with all my siblings, Rajan, Ajay and Sanjeev, my sisters-in-law, Rittu, Selena and Kajal, the extended family and friends. It was a memorable time as we revelled in the togetherness during the heartwarming celebrations. There were two parties in one week and both were equally pleasurable.

However, sometimes happiness has sadness lurking behind it as it was during that time that I received the news of my mother suffering from pulmonary fibrosis, a lung condition with no effective cure. I was informed of the degenerative nature of the condition and it was then that I had to think no further. It was a vital moment for me that was convincing me to turn the page once more.

With reality hitting me hard, I returned to Delhi holding a crystallised vision of my future. It was the beginning of July and Sonakshi and I had six weeks to go before we wound up and left for New York to settle her down in her new life in NYU.

I, unhesitatingly, announced my departure to my family, friends, Guruji's disciples and the city of Delhi itself that was responsible for all my problems as well as all my solutions. Delhi, one of the most polluted cities in the world, had purified my life lending it a clarity that no other city in the world could have given me. It afforded me my life lessons and subsequently the answers. It gave me thorns but then showered me with roses in abundance. Above all, it gave me the gift of Guruji, the Eternal Light that would hopefully travel with me to the West. He had commanded me to do satsangs before He discarded His physical garb and I wondered now how that would be possible with people's lack of receptivity.

I developed a strong affinity with Delhi but I was as clear as day about not wanting to live in any regret. Hence, to be by my mother's side was the only place on earth for me. I had instinctively known that my decision to leave the East and to settle back in the West was the most responsible one. More importantly, it was the right one for my mother. I spring-cleaned my home from dawn to dusk in the same way as I had cleaned up my life—scrupulously and superbly well. I was about to leave it in an orderly and organised fashion with memories still residing there to fill up the emptiness of my spacious apartment.

One of the many miracles that Guruji had performed was indeed making me fall deeply in love with Delhi and post-divorce it became even deeper as I viewed it in a different context. What is love? Love is this character who has a split personality. It has the ideal in it as well as the real. It carries the unpredictability of a destination that is neither realised nor reached. Hence, love is a journey to embrace but not to own, as it has no destination, no permanent abode. Love resides within each of us, so carry its torch to illuminate others' lives wherever you go.

My closest friends and my extended family of cousins, from the beginning of July till the time I departed, towards the middle of August, hosted farewell dinners that will never be forgotten till my memory fades at the age of 120! Every afternoon, after being treated for lunch, I was subsequently treated for dinner! In between, there were coffee and high-tea treats too! I was hugely moved by the emotion of it and by now my stomach was also moving in a new direction!

'Friendship is precious, not only in the shade, but in the sunshine of life, and thanks to a benevolent arrangement the greater part of life is sunshine,' observed Thomas Jefferson.

Each time we were together, we laughed heartily and shared our lives and victories and how far we had all come. For the first time, I realised that I was laughing with my friends from a place of real happiness and no longer needed to 'wear the happy mask.' The transformational power of time cannot be underestimated, as it really was happily ever laughter! Guruji had injected in me an unmistakable zeal for life and for love and that was being mirrored back into my life through my family, friends and my Gurparivaar (Guruji's family).

I can write chapter and verse on each of my friend's, family's and sangat's attributes and how they selflessly contributed to my recovery and revival whilst orchestrating a happy future for me. They really are angels on earth, descended straight from heaven to enable me to first walk, then sprint! They, along with many other well-wishers, friends and family, redefined love for me. Love as it is in the dictionary, is an intense feeling, a deep romantic or sexual attachment to someone. My definition is an intense feeling of deep respect and compassion for the other that is synonymous with pure love. This kind of love is bound to give a happy ending and the happily-ever-after need not come only after a divorce!

'How beautiful a day can turn when kindness touches it,' remarked George Elliston.

Friends are God's way of taking care of us and family is God's way of loving us. Whenever a shadow of doubt spread across my day covering me with a dismal feeling, I looked around me and observed many layers of love and care engulf my life. I knew then that He will walk with me till the end of time, be it here in Delhi, or there in England.

Winston Churchill had said, 'Never, never, never give up,' and this sentiment was echoed by my truest friends and close family members who got me back on the road again. I thanked each of my beloved friends and cousins with a small gift and a sincere prayer in my heart for their never-ending kindness and happiness. Over time, they all connected with Guruji and visited the temple regularly. That was more pleasing to see than anything else. I was eternally grateful to them for their boundless support and I was eternally indebted to the One who had made all this possible. After the satisfying storm of the partying, there had to be a gratifying calm of Guruji's temple where Lord Shiva reigns supreme and where peace reigns my heart. It is all about balance after all.

22

The Final Dose

We all die but not all of us really live. I believe
I am on the path to learning the art of living.

Author

My heart seized with humility, I visited Guruji's temple for the final dose of strength before my departure from the city that schooled me to hold my own. It was a calm day with a slightly overcast sky, its mood corresponding with my own. The mysticism and the healing power of the aura of the temple were embedded in me. The huge majestic trees lined the side of the walking track stretching their branches to provide shelter to those who sat in meditation. There was an air of comfort too and I couldn't help but wonder about the clean start I was about to make. Faith is such that we don't really know where it's taking us or where we are going with it but its sacred commitment keeps us sure and steady, giving us purpose and focus. I felt like an accomplished woman who had successfully rebuilt her life after a major downfall. Deep inside my spirit, I was finally joyous and life was filled with beautiful possibilities, not ugly dread. Some of the big 'life' questions were answered here and prepared me for the life I was about to face.

It was the last Monday before my departure and there were several disciples, old and new, who requested me to speak, so I sat on the lawns comfortably and spoke endlessly about my experiences after being enveloped by our beloved Guruji's love. We gain our blessings by sharing. As I spoke, I found more and more people gather around me to listen with bated breath about my own blessings as well as the wider message. Most of us get our answers from another. Hence, what has always been brought to light is that all disciples are mentors to each other and mediums of Guruji's expression and we are all equally driven to seek the truth about our own lives.

Most listeners were newcomers and it was their declaration of collective faith that moved me the most, as without ever having met Him, they believe in Him. The old disciples had believed that Guruji had brought the curtain down on their faith after He discarded His human form until they realised His absolute presence in their lives. With the shopping list of benefits and blessings, they continued their journey by engaging themselves in selfless work in the temple, be it in the form of cooking, cleaning or sharing their experiences. Each seva had its own significance.

In recent months, I also took on board that by reaching out to others, you create ripples of joy in their lives whilst you annihilate your own sorrow. Guruji always advocated the significance of sharing and then would teasingly state that humans are hoarders and they don't even like to share their blessings! In the same breath, He stated, 'Delhi society and the world at large is in dire straits as far as their core values are concerned. People are losing their moral compass, so it is imperative for you to inspire others through your own change. Faith needs to be the central element to uphold society and to keep people connected.'

One of the old disciples who was well entrenched in faith and knew me since the time I first arrived here 13 years ago, looked astonishingly at me and said, 'You have become so beautiful since coming to Guruji. Please don't misunderstand me. Please take this in the right spirit but it's almost like the ugly duckling has been transformed into a beautiful swan. I know you had a terrible skin disease and people used to avert their gaze on seeing you. You really are Guruji's miracle and whenever I see you, my faith is restored. I have heard you speak about your ongoing and growing journey umpteen times but each time it feels new and there is something to draw from it. Thank you.'

Needless to say, I did take this woman's statement in the spirit in which it was intended as I too would avoid my own reflection but I looked directly at it now and said each time, 'I love you, the woman in the mirror, but never forget the One who has brought about this miraculous change.'

I had many aspects of my life fixed since then including my crushed spirit. I also knew, however, that the bereaved and broken me that wore the grief-lined face even after it had been healed was now dead and buried and I was viewing myself not as the victim but the victor. The reflection of the woman I now saw in the mirror was a courageous, strong and happy one. The past, as I understand it from the karmic theory, was possibly *meant to be* but now I engaged in situations that were *meant for me!*

I appreciated this woman's honesty and revelled in the thought of having become a symbol of hope for her and for others. I was sufficiently blessed to have become a representation of Guruji's infinite Supremacy. I had become a beacon for others and I enjoyed the role that Guruji Himself had allotted me. He said on discarding His physical garb, 'You must talk to people and inspire them as there are many who live in the dark just as you did, but you came into light and as a blessed human, it is your moral duty to enable others to seek light too. Times ahead are volatile and there will be instability on all fronts: relationships, finances or health. Times ahead are not good, Anita, and your responsibility is to spread light through your satsangs. I have given you my full blessings, go and do your work and be happy.'

I glanced at the beautiful disciples and acknowledged the fact that beauty lay with in each one of us and the ugliness can only be eradicated with the touch of the Supremely Beautiful One. I believed it then and I believe it now with ever more conviction that real love and friendship are possible only with the blessings of the Supreme One.

On meeting this fine-looking woman, I was reminded of where I came from and where I had arrived. I reflected on of how resilient the human spirit is as it is revitalised to power the life we want to live. I had turned an important corner that was vital to my well-being and to a healthier and happier future. I had access to the past to draw value from it and be deeply grateful to all the incredible events that led to my most satisfying present. I thanked my past as it was because of it that I could appreciate my present. Had I had the courage to retain a photograph of myself then to compare the 'before and after', the quantum leap would be evident. Having said that, whilst I was spring-cleaning my home before my exit, I came across a few photographs that Sanjeev's friend Amit had taken of me immediately after my separation. We had gone out for dinner and although I was healed much before that of my skin disease, my heart was still very much ailing. I appeared careworn; neither the palpable grief nor the emotions could be concealed as I wrestled with feelings of self-pity and self-defeat.

How far had I come? On that day, I had probably felt happiness was beyond my reach but just as the sun rose day after day, so did I. I rose and rose until the sun began to clear the horizon and its radiance fell on my life. With every passing season, I became more seasoned! I am glad that Amit had documented that moment, as today I can marvel at my progress. If during that phase of my life you had looked up the word 'sadness' in the dictionary, you would see a picture of me! Happiness for me has taken on a new meaning. I have learnt to let go and also learnt that it's not about trying to fix something broken; it's about starting again and creating something far better.

I thanked the lady at the temple whilst we sipped on tea and bit into our samosas (Indian savoury) that was not only good on the palate but also good on the soul. Healing through food was one of Guruji's many prescriptions. Whilst savouring the blessed food, I broke the unsavoury news of my departure that week. I explained my move was predominantly for my ailing mother. Since the lady at the temple was an old disciple, I also searched for some answers to explain this imminent change by carefully reading her face as if they were written there. After a few minutes of reflection, she spoke, her piercing gaze resembling Guruji's as if she were looking straight into my soul in the same manner that He used to, 'You have a higher calling. Your mother needs you and Guruji is with you even there. You will also find and make more disciples but we will miss you deeply as you really have inspired our faith and devotion. I am sure you will do the same out there in the West and you must. You are lucky as you can have two homes plus the temple, which makes three, but then you are blessed and that is clear to see, Anita. Guruji has given your life a new direction. Jai Guruji (Hail Guruji).'

'She embraced me with warmth that locked me in the moment. It could have been 10 seconds or hours but it had the significance of a lifetime. Each of us gets our answers through the other and she with her grace reassured me that destiny was at work.

Before I succumbed to tears, I gently left her side to inch towards the inside of the temple. I bowed in deep veneration before Guruji's life-sized photograph. I prayed for my mother's protection and to be able to give her the love and care that I deprived her of in all these years that I lived away from her. Let me give her a lifetime of love for the rest of her days. Let me cook for her too! That was something I hadn't really done much of out here, but there it would be different. I would garnish all my

149

dishes with unmeasured love to feed her soul. I said a little prayer of gratitude and then I was filled with the euphoric sensation of pure, deep and desire-less love. I came to that moment where I fell in love. My energies were transformed and changed. All my senses were animated here and both the philosopher and the poet in me expressed a measure of gratitude to life and to existence.

'This awe-inspiring temple for me is my first and last wonder of the world and I sit here in deep gratitude. I thank You endlessly for the health, wealth, my happy, healthy and successful daughters, and for the opportunity to start all over again. I thank You in advance for all the great times to come, as I know they will with You in my life. I know I have done it and will continue to do many great things but it's all You. The love I feel here with You is matchless and I have never experienced such pure love anywhere else. You really are my cure-all and be-all. Come with me to England!'

There was a sudden blaze of emotion as I turned my tear-streaked face to the floor before I rose again after several meditative moments and walked out to the lawns. I passed many more disciples and nodded at them in acknowledgement. Some wished me well and others who didn't know me, simply smiled. They were all my family and this was my world.

I walked out to the front of the temple to get a panoramic view of its unspoken beauty and its unyielding divinity. If there is a heaven on earth, guess what? I've seen it!

23

The Lesson

A life without cause
is a life without effect.

Barbarella

As I was making my exit from the spellbinding temple that I would re-visit again and again other than in my memory, a thought entered my mind. As a child, I had always wanted to reside in India even though I was born and brought up in England. I believe I came here for the purpose of soul-growth that was probably not going to happen in England. Post-divorce, I used to sit and make sense of the disarray but then through faith I learnt that it is OK for none of it to make sense. I learnt, I grew and I evolved. I was taken under the wing of a Higher Power who set me on the path of my liberation and salvation. Self-realisation is too big a word for me but I had realised a sufficient amount about myself to gain a clearer vision of my life ahead. I may not have got a fair deal to

151

begin with but I got the real deal in the end. I seriously couldn't even begin to count my blessings. The fact that my daughters were on the right road was a sure sign of all the good that was being steered into my life by Guruji.

As for my personal growth, my role as a wife of 18 years was to tend to my former husband's needs, to make things work for him. In the aftermath of my divorce, I learnt to make it work for me. After being adrift for a few years subsequently, I learnt to embrace the person I was as well as my life experiences. Today, my life had gained momentum and I was truly comfortable in my own skin. What I am today is the sum total of everything I have experienced, good and bad, and I am glad for the tireless self-reinvention. The acrimony towards my past had dissolved and the tangible evidence of my newfound happiness was the radiance on my face that many people commented on. The breakdown of my marriage led to a breakthrough in my personal and spiritual growth, giving my life beauty and matter. What I lost in youth, I gained in substance. I have reframed the canvas of my past in a new context as I move on to another dimension of life. The cold war had truly ended as the days of peace and happiness were here.

I recollected the very first time I met Guruji and how I fell wondrously at His sublime feet. From that moment on, He had wrapped His love around me like a warm, protective blanket to keep me from the cold of the world. He always said that we must take off our 'ego' our 'ifs and 'buts' and our 'pre-conceived notions' along with our shoes before entering His domain. Faith and logic don't make very good friends, so leave the latter out to surrender to a higher power.

I would be re-visiting this place other than in my recollection as it recharges my spirit. This Shiva temple is a transitional place where we are constantly changing and evolving and the constant love of Guruji is ever-present. Hence, to regularly visit the temple keeps us in harmony with faith. Faith itself is delicate and can get side-tracked but through regular practice, we are able to nudge ourselves back. He is still awakening His disciples, old and new, from their slumber. In fact, Guruji used to say that there is no old or new as we are not aware of how many lifetimes of search finally gets us connected to Him, the divine. His heart still beats here amongst His longing disciples and it is these sensibilities that are felt and experienced by other disciples all the time. His fingerprints are all over the temple and on just one visit, He gathers us in His benign clasp. People are flooding in today as the sangat is growing the world over by leaps and bounds. It is a declaration of the collective faith of believing in something even when you can't see it. I cannot see Him but I feel Him in the subtle nuances of my life and in my heart that has become a deep ocean of spiritual surrender.

In spite of the highs and lows, the twists and turns of my life, my sense of aloneness had turned into nurturing peace that filled my soul. Before I sat in my car, I made a statement, a declaration: 'I am at peace and all is well within my soul and I feel a deep joy in my heart.' The words reverberated in my mind all the way home along with a sense of unspoken acknowledgement of the victory inside of me of having come out the other side a complete winner. To measure your happiness today, take your negative canvas of the past and place it next to your positive canvas of your present and you'll appreciate the contrast.

My door will be open and my lights on in case He, Guruji decides to come visit me.

24

My Mother

Life began with waking up
and loving my mother's face.

George Eliot

I held a prayer meeting on 12th August to celebrate my father's birthday that was on the 11th. I prayed in earnest for my mother's recovery too.

It was an incredibly successful satsang for my father in which my family, close relatives and closest friends were also present. That made it all the more meaningful, with my father's heart also beating amongst us. It was he who was propelling me forward to take care of my mother, his beloved wife. I just knew it!

More than a few tears were shed and several promises were made by my friends and relatives to visit me in England. Fewer still were convinced that I would be back sooner than I realised. In my heart of hearts, I knew it was time and though goodbyes are hard to digest, I had no regrets about my past choices or my current ones. I must do that which must be done. It was all or nothing and I was prepared to give my all to my mother. I marvelled at life for giving me a second chance to love the most sacred figure in our lives and the one we take most for granted. I was going to be hands-on mother to my mother!

On the morning of my departure, under an early morning monsoon sky, I locked up my apartment of four years. It carried both light and heavy emotions that turned into enduring memories. Before I stepped out of the building, I went upstairs to my neighbours place to express my gratitude for their unfailing support and endless generosity. Then I hugged my teary-eyed domestic help before I bid farewell to the land in which I had grown by leaps and bounds, and which had taken away my identity, my self-respect and my dignity 22 years earlier only to return it with more substance 22 years later. Each ounce of everything I lost was regained and much more than can be quantified. Yet another chapter was about to begin. In fact, there are many more verses and volumes waiting to be written.

Such are destiny's ways and who can ever figure that out. I landed on Indian soil in August at the age of 22 and precisely 22 years later again in August, I was bidding it my farewell. So much had been lost and much more had been regained but then whoever said I was not transporting it all back with me to Manchester, England.

Here I was in the newly built Delhi international airport still in its final stages. It was being prepared for the Commonwealth Games to be hosted in the city in October, 2010. I was pleasantly surprised by its size and scale and its high standards. Seeing WH Smith there was a sign of how close I was to home! I smiled as I recalled my childhood memories of buying my stationery in WH Smith in Altrincham, Cheshire, which was walking distance from my father's residence. It was practically my second home as a teenager as I had a passion for buying stationery but never used it. Buy and hoard.com!

I was grossly overweight as my luggage carried everything from my memories of my treasured friends, the vivid image and spirit of my Guruji's temple, my family's boundless love, particularly my baby brother Sanjeev's. I knew life would not be easy without him, my caring neighbours who were indeed the ready-made family I recently got acquainted with and the infinite wisdom gained from my experiences in India, the land where my shattered dreams were mended and taken to an inconceivably higher level.

I developed a deep respect for the muddled city of Delhi as it was here in its chaos that I had found my order. I clicked a photograph of all my life's events here and placed it in the frame of my memory. I would download certain images as and when I sat alone in a reflective mood. It's strange how we don't remember days but we all remember moments. No matter how far we travel, memories will always accompany us.

After embarking on the plane, I sat with my stomach churning in anticipation of the impending angst and excitement of starting again and being afforded the opportunity to wrap layers of my love around my mother. My heart was pounding with the anxiety of not knowing how my life would unfold in the West. Of one thing, though, I was certain: I would leave no stone unturned in showering my mother with my unbounded love and warmth. With my love and Guruji's blessings, she would regain her health to live joyously into the ripe old age of witnessing her grandchildren's big fat Indian weddings!

25

Sonakshi

Continuity gives us roots; change gives us branches
letting us stretch and grow and reach new heights.

Pauline R Kezer

Both Anishka and Sonakshi are indeed extraordinary girls as their
indomitable spirit is what motivated me all along my journey.
They weathered the storm much more gracefully than I did, and
my overwhelming guilt and failure were ironed out with their
strength and courage. I was powerless and could not bring the
course of events that were unfolding to a quick and peaceful end.
Even though I may have written the script, I had not directed the
story that had gone terribly wrong.

I found Anishka to be particularly grounded. In her presence,
my mind did not race at 100 miles an hour as her very calm
disposition calmed my inner storm too. She also had a very

balanced view of every situation. Sonakshi, on the other hand, was more emotional and had the gift to unburden me with her humour and light-hearted nature. She was more chirpy and cheerful, so with both of them around, I never felt emotionally bankrupt. My despair, then, was as clear as day whereas their hope was as solid as a rock. They were a perfect blend of love, compassion and endurance and my days were never bland with them around. I can never compensate for all the pain I may have caused my daughters despite my best efforts, values and intentions but I can pray that they are showered with so much more happiness in their lives that the misery is erased from it. Through rain they have learnt to value sunshine. I do believe that whatever happens in our lives is for our personal evolution, so they too are learning through life's vicissitudes. 'Life is the art of drawing without an eraser,' avers John W Gardner.

Despite the hardships of their parents' divorce, my girls did not succumb to its challenges or submit to the inevitable emotional suffering. Guruji had shielded them well. They dealt effectively with their loss by filling their time and their vacuum with friends, schoolwork, family commitments, their own goals and aspirations. They never lost sight of their direction in life, which was most commendable under the adverse circumstances. In fact, their bearings became even clearer after my separation and studying in the US was a non-negotiable decision. Their vision of the future was clear and it was most reassuring for me to know that my girls were most capable of taking charge. I admired their resilience and their contagious enthusiasm. In effect, they understood more than I did about trusting our instincts and taking chances after losing, finding happiness and finally cherishing the good times and letting go of the not-so-good ones. I was learning much about being a spur-of-the-moment and sprightly individual from both my girls.

Anishka slipped into her new life in LA like a hand in a glove. She assumed her new role as an undergrad student effortlessly and easily. Now it was Sonakshi's turn to leave as she gained admission in NYU. She was about to start her freshman year and my pride knew no bounds as this is what I had affirmed since I had believed in it. I was happy and sad, as is usually the case, as soon I would be faced with ENT (Empty Nest Test).

Children grow and go away from their parents. I was their facilitator. My role was to prepare them to face life with confidence, making them self-sufficient and self-reliant. In the bargain, I became redundant. The transition is never a painless one. I made them independent of me but I will certainly never be independent of them. Hence, the empty nest syndrome shall remain forever!

Sonakshi and I spent three days with my mother in Manchester before we boarded our flight to New York. It was here that I felt Guruji had loosened His grip on me as I was filled with a deep void after settling Sonakshi down at her university apartment with a very heavy heart.

I returned unaccompanied to the hotel where I was to spend three more nights sans my daughter. I cried buckets as I deeply missed her. Then I realised how profoundly I missed Anishka too. Reality hit me quite hard as my positive outlook soon turned negative on realising that now, if truth be told, I was actually alone. The emptiness would need to be filled and I simply hoped and prayed that Guruji had road-mapped my life. Else, I would lose my way.

It was at this point that I texted a disciple of Guruji's in Delhi for a potential contact in NYC who followed Guruji. I didn't think the person would respond as I sat in quiet anticipation in my hotel room, staring blankly at my laptop screen! Within moments I received a couple of contacts and my remaining three days in the city were unbelievably pleasurable with Guruji's ever-pervading blessings so evidently clear. We spoke endlessly about Guruji as we went on tours, sipped tea and ate like there was no tomorrow. The fraternity and brotherhood was bound by unconditional love as I had never met these people, yet they were more than family. Such are Guruji's ways of teaching us to trust again and to love without conditions. One of the disciples, Ganga, shared the importance of me finding a life partner too and I just shuddered at the idea, almost brushing her off. She insisted and stated: 'Within a year, there ought to be someone in your life and you will be very happy.' Was Guruji speaking through her? I had heard that He works in close collaboration with His devotees. For me, however, He is the one who plays centrestage. No one can come close to the love that I feel for Him, my Guruji.

My focus for the moment was my mother and I needed to return to Manchester now that Sonakshi was smoothly settling down into her new life. Her sociable nature had already attracted a few friends before I departed. Her chapter had begun as mine too was about to and I knew I didn't need to worry about her. I had received the reassurance from my newfound friends in New York that Guruji was always watching over me, my daughters and my mother and that we would always be protected. Guruji used to state, 'By you coming to me, your entire family is blessed.'

There is never an exact 'how to' in life for any aspect of it but I do know that in all that went terribly wrong, I did something terrifically right for my daughters to turn out the way they have! They taught me to 'look ahead' and that is precisely what I was about to do. I had crawled, stood, walked, sprinted. Now I was ready to soar high.

26

Manchester

Life is a foreign language;
all men mispronounce it.

Christopher Morley

I returned to Manchester as a foreigner! I felt like a stranger here after being reborn in India. I had been away for far too long and had almost forgotten its many attributes. Manchester, my birthplace, also gave birth to the world's first computer—designed in Manchester University.

Mr Rolls met Mr Royce in Midland Hotel here in Manchester to join hands to produce the world-renowned ultra luxury Rolls Royce in Crewe factory 25 miles away. Both Bentley and Rolls Royce are manufactured here.

On the fringe of Manchester was my mother's home in an area called Bowdon, which was also home to many Manchester United Premium League players. Within half a mile of my mother's home were two national trust properties—Dunham Park and Tatton Park—that I hoped to visit regularly if there ever would be respite from the unrelenting rain that the city was subjected to. Another interesting feature within the sight of Bowdon, Cheshire, was the world's largest radio telescope in Jodrell Bank. Then there was the Manchester Art Gallery too that would keep my creative juices flowing.

Here I was with my mother in her new apartment and her housekeeper, Monica, to maintain it. Gosh! I needed a life manual again to indicate the way! I floated on a sea of questions that questioned my existence. It wasn't going to be smooth sailing emotionally as I was now away from my two daughters, the home I had grown to love, my family, friends, my sangat and the temple along with the buzz of Delhi. Comparisons are odious. To start afresh, I needed to view Manchester for what it was with all its inherent attributes. Aloo gobi earned the respected title of 'dish of the day' almost everyday as I tried my hand at it for the very first time after my return. On my second attempt, I half paid attention to it whilst cooking it as I realised the lack of creativity involved! The aroma of the dish filled me with the nostalgia of my childhood and I realised that life had taken me full circle. To begin with, the fresh air here was most inviting, an element I had deeply missed in the years than I stayed away. I inhaled deep the air I had been deprived of. Once again, I was inhaling the air of freedom and renewed possibilities. The canvas was mine to paint on and the colours I would splash on were also my choice. What a liberating thought!

After being in Manchester for a few days, my positively liberating thoughts returned rapidly to what I had left behind. The only way is forward, I know, and I was undeniably engaging myself in the most meaningful and morally correct deed of taking my ailing mother under my wing, bonding with my brothers with whom I had barely spent quality time after my long absence reconnecting with my most accommodating sisters-in-law and rediscovering the friends from whom I had moved on. A mountain of a challenge lay ahead of me but I carefully and scrupulously took one step at a time with contained emotions. That is the beauty of life: you are to live it only step by step, which takes you into your future that opens up new possibilities. Not entirely true!

Practically every night, I questioned the drastic change that had come about in my life and in the mornings, after customarily lighting a candle before Guruji's photograph that sat quietly in my bedroom, I would ask Him audibly, 'What's the plan, Guruji?' Turning a different corner does not necessarily have smooth edges to it but once you've made the turn, your perspective does change after a point.

I silently missed the road I had travelled on in recent years and now I had to navigate my life into a new direction, which, over the months, I was finding increasingly difficult.

I began cooking a dish daily for my mother to gratify her palate and to satisfy my conscience. The smile in my mother's eyes on savouring my dish was worth my moving back in with her despite the uncertainty that lay ahead. I felt alone and lonely and my dishes were soon going to be garnished with anything but love if life didn't throw up a surprise. I considered many options including picking up the paintbrush and splashing colours on a brand new canvas but to do even that, I felt emotionally immobilised.

Many months elapsed before I knelt before Guruji to plead with Him to reveal my life's purpose. There had to be more for me to be and do. My divorce had thrown life out of gear for a while but then I took charge and here I was beginning to feel the same way despite the presence of continuous support. 'I am at no age to experiment with life Guruji, so please give me a clear direction since I am utterly lost! Give me some signposts and a navigation system that guide me to my purpose. Please and Thank You!'

I had many emotional breakdowns with just Him and me in my room until the sun rose again one fine autumn afternoon when a friend of mine bbmed me from India asking me to contact Guruji's disciples living in Manchester! My first response was 'Wow!' followed by a skeptical thought—they must be residing somewhere on the remote outskirts. After speaking to them excitedly as though I had found a long-lost lover, I learnt that they were residing precisely 10 minutes away! Unbelievable! Their joy also knew no bounds as they were keen to initiate satsangs as soon as I had found my feet. I reassured them that the only way to find my feet was to start satsangs right away. To plan them, we met regularly over meals first at their place, then at mine where I subjected them to my lack of culinary skills!

Guruji also sent my Guru sister Anisha and her husband Gautam to stay with me in Manchester for a few brief days before we all took off to Algarve, Portugal for a vacation of a lifetime. On arriving at Algarve, at my father's stunningly plush villa overlooking a perfectly green golf course, we hired a car and drove to Seville, Spain for lunch, came back to Algarve, then the following day drove to Lisbon where we stayed overnight after visiting Fatima where Mother Mary had manifested herself. The entire 15-day vacation was a dream and I couldn't thank Guruji enough for the respite. They left and I soon got into a mundane routine of walks, cooking and joining Apple one-to-one course that enabled me to grasp the many features and functions of my laptop.

No two days are the same as life takes many unpredictable turns. My brother Sanjay fell terribly sick with a disease that attacked his immune system. He was critical. I, along with the family, was depressed though my youngest brother Sanjeev was optimistic about his recovery. The doctors were frighteningly close to giving up hope on him. The most dreary cloud hung over our forlorn family for an entire month. Sanjeev flew over from Delhi to Manchester to be with him to uplift our spirits with the power of his faith. He discreetly placed Guruji's photograph under Sanjay's hospital pillow: 'Guruji is with all of us, so Sanjay will recover in no time. He is totally protected so no need to get anxious. He too will someday believe in His supremacy as will our other brothers and family members.'

After careful examination of my forlorn face, he stated that I ought to be the pillar of faith for the family after having come out of such ghastly situations. Surely there was no room for doubt after the miraculous turn of many favourable events in my own life. I nodded in agreement and realised that I was actually lacking in faith by allowing negative thoughts to dominate my mind.

Faith and positive thinking ought to be the driving force even in the gloomiest situation. Seeing my otherwise active and athletic brother lying helplessly in the hospital bed did make me question life but soon Sanjeev turned around my and everyone else's attitude.

Sanjay always had a positive mental make-up that made him excel in every sphere of his life. A health fanatic too, he consumed only that which contained enormous health benefits even if it was not the most beneficial to his taste buds! What made me disbelieve, initially, is the questioning expression on his otherwise certain and confidant countenance. On Sanjeev's arrival, however, my negativity dissolved and my faith was restored.

Our negative thinking blocks out the positive energy that otherwise permeates our lives if we remain open to it. Guruji used to advocate the significance of having a sunny disposition even when there was a heavy downpour to allow goodness to come into our lives. Be strong, courageous and God-loving, and the divine will definitely see you through.

Once Sanjay recovered miraculously from his ghastly illness, he made vacation plans to Tenerife with his wife, Kajal, his children, Sanjeev, my mother and I over Christmas. My mother's pulmonary specialist had resisted her travel plans to begin with but, of course, with Sanjeev's undying confidence, she accompanied us only to have a whale of a time with all of us. Guruji was at work, as always!

In my four months of being in Manchester, I had already travelled to two most exotic destinations. This really translates the power of faith and the prayers answered by Him on my asking Him to make me travel far and wide and as frequently as possible!

Living in Manchester became much easier after discovering the art of knowing how to live there: frequent travelling, staying busy with constructive work and a positive mental make-up that gives you infinite possibilities to excel in no matter where you are. I began writing too. Then in the New Year, on arriving back to UK after our Christmas vacation in Canary Islands, I flew back to Delhi at the drop of a hat literally. I had barely caught my breath when my younger daughter Sonakshi demanded I fly back as she and her sister Anishka were there for their winter break for a couple of weeks. I booked my ticket to Delhi the day I landed from Tenerife and left the following day joyously after getting the green signal from my mother. I needed to know that she would be fine in my absence and I instinctively knew that she would. 'Guruji please protect her.'

After having the time of my life for those two weeks with my daughters, friends and the sangat, in addition to experiencing many subtle miracles performed by the Supreme Magician, I returned home on a high and that is when I called up Guruji's sangat in Manchester to fix a day when we would initiate a prayer meeting. We expected not more than 10 people and had over 25! Sabina, my childhood friend, was in her element in the satsang as she had met Guruji many years back in His physical presence. She was most connected and confident about the prospect of holding regular satsangs here in Manchester. I knew that people would become receptive in times to come, as the need of the hour was to connect. It was a very promising beginning. After that, my mother began to believe in the power of faith and insisted that I pray to Guruji for her to be granted permission from her doc to visit India. It was kind of unreasonable considering he was clearly against her travelling to Tenerife. India was much further away. Besides the distance, Delhi's pollution would do her no good, so it was inadvisable for her to entertain this thought. Then I spoke to Sanjeev for reassurance and he was his customary confident self! 'Yes, yes, please do come over and stay for a few months! Mother can even attend satsangs with us and we'll take her to Guruji's ashram!'

The advice seemed pretty far-fetched but then everything in Guruji's domain is improbable and ridiculously unrealistic. After taking a semi-convincing go-ahead from the doc, my mother and I merrily flew to Delhi where satsangs played centrestage during my several months stay there. In between, I even flew to Kuwait where I was asked to speak at length to over 600 people about my most sublime journey with my beloved Guruji. Love simply overflowed as I interacted with people who too were on their journey with Him. We all spoke more or less the same language and were gazing in the same direction. There is a certain collective energy that is generated by people in sync with one another. No conflicts, no confusion and no contradictions. There was only harmony, the result of a collective consciousness that pervaded the environment. I was totally in my element during the eight days that I was there, sharing and giving and allowing the energy to flow without restraint. The sharing was honest and authentic with no flowery language or false perceptions. I told it the way it was and it was that unerring accuracy of my experiences that brought about a positively emotional response. True love permeated a roomful of believers who sighed with the relief of knowing that they are on their path of truth and happiness as all my experiences were relatable to them one way or another. Most faces light up with renewed faith and hope when Guruji's love is spoken of and my personal journey certainly endorsed His supremacy. True love cannot be found where it doesn't exist and it cannot be hidden where it does.

Human issues are, after all, common to all men and women. They may vary in degrees but they are relatable to all ears that listen. After a point of talking on the microphone whilst observing peoples responses, I realised the commonality between them and

I when several heads nodded in agreement as if I were relating their story. It's the shared destiny of a collective humanity that makes people relate to one another's issues. Human suffering crosses religious, social and cultural boundaries. It is dissolved only through compassion and love that has no bias as no one in Guruji's terrain passes judgment on the other as we are all there to facilitate the other's journey through the power of faith. Guruji used to state time and again, 'All godliness comes from the same source.' Faith is the only universal language that binds people and draws them to their ultimate goal.

I realised that my purpose that was unfolding before me was to reach out to others through my very own blessings and the grace showered upon me during every second of my rebirth. I began to believe that this new-found role was entrusted to me by Guruji Himself who stated before leaving His physical garb that I must inspire others through satsangs. Through one's own blessings, we must learn to share. By doing so, we alleviate the pain others may be suffering.

My purpose was becoming increasingly clear to me at this point in my life—March 2011—almost 5 years post-separation.

27

The Power of Faith

Weave in faith
and God will find the thread.

Kabir Das

He, my Guruji, rooted out fear from the very fabric of my being. He transformed unmistaken doubt into unerring faith, dissolved all my preconceived notions about Him as a mere guru and my foregone conclusion about His magnificence.

The answers are far bigger than the questions and no matter how articulate one may be or how extended one's vocabulary, when it comes to explaining His greatness, words fail us. It is the experiential and the practical that count, not merely the simple theory.

I make myself look adequately foolish when I rule out logic and speak of irrational faith and how it drives us ahead on the road of life. I aspire to be the paragon of faith and what it stands for through my behaviour. It is not what is inside us but what we do that defines us. My way of seeing and understanding things have taken a turn for the better. I no longer dwell on fear that is translated into belief that things will go wrong!

With my limited vision and understanding, I have endeavoured to share my most incredible journey with you, the reader, incredulous as it may sound. The endeavour throughout my writing has been to enable you to perhaps gain insight into your own lives and for me to render you strength to pass the trying phases of your lives with the understanding that whatever happens is ultimately for our own soul growth, for our personal evolution. When a divine being such as Guruji touches our lives, we are transformed internally and externally. Spirituality that is synonymous with simplicity, silence and surrender, takes over to give us the strength to surmount every storm.

What is clear to my mind is that it was darkness that compelled my spirit to seek the Light of Divinity. Hence, I am in deep gratitude for all the misfortune that befell me as it was only then that I sought the pure and unending love of my Guruji. In hindsight, the pain that I underwent then was the catalyst that brought me onto this path of truth. I have learnt the life lessons without wallowing in self-pity. Rather, with the wisdom that has strengthened me from within, I have learnt the lesson of self-love and self-acceptance. When we honestly begin to respect the God-force within us, then the good gravitates towards us, expanding our aura and protecting us from negative elements. Like attracts like and what I seem to do is attract like-minded people who are on the journey.

On travelling with my Guruji, I was able to connect the dots to make good sense of my life. He restored my faith in goodness and its ability to erase negativity. Integrity and honesty have command and authority. He taught me to stand tall in the face of adversity and every challenging situation.

He taught me acceptance, particularly of my karma and subsequently, the art of surrendering myself to Him for the change of that karma.

Guruji stated that to become aware of the God-force within was the only way to wake up from slumber and to live with absolute acceptance and appreciation. His grace and His healing enabled me to tiptoe towards my decision to break my already collapsed marriage, then to sprint towards normality post-divorce. He restored my self-belief, getting me back on track in relatively less time than it would have otherwise taken if He were not in my life. He swiftly filled the gaps in my life to afford me a feeling of completeness.

The path of spirituality is never smooth sailing, particularly when your Guru tests your patience and perseverance endlessly but mercifully! On meeting me, He probably scanned my soul and wondered where to begin with its purification. He may have felt that He had an awful deal of work to do!

Guruji's philosophy was especially simple. Sitting in His aura everyday for my healing on every possible level from my physical, mental and emotional to my spiritual, was both beneficial and blissful. Beyond a point in time, I became addicted to His love. Every evening, as soon as the clock struck 6 pm, I parked myself anxiously outside His abode and waited rather restlessly to be called in to have the divine tea with Him before the rest of the disciples settled themselves down at the allotted time of 7 pm.

The power of faith and the power of love together healed and transformed my being and my life. I would unfailingly sit beside Him to listen to the shabads that I vaguely understood; I ate langar and listened attentively to the other devotees experiences on how they benefited from surrendering their lives to Guruji. This, along with having unadulterated faith and devotion, was the order of the day. It was so simple sitting with Him and feeling His vibrations, as the experience was elevating and enjoyable. I am certain that His mere vibrations were changing mine to

171

bring me onto a higher frequency. After He was done doing what He had to, there was a sea change in my perspective. My attitude towards myself, and the world at large, changed radically. From then to now, I am convinced that I am not the same person.

As I stated earlier, the path of spirituality is never an easy one but it is most rewarding and fulfilling. Where faith begins, logic ends, so sometimes you can look like the biggest fool speaking about your miracles. I, for one, was the biggest oddball in my social circle and perhaps in my own family until there was evident change in my being and in my life. Truth has its own gravity and no one needs to light a torch to see the sun. Hence, Guruji's Supremacy spoke for itself through the light He shed not only on my life but on a large number of people. He breathed new life into their days of dejection and discord.

Today, His following has and is still growing across continents in various countries, encompassing many cities. His divine light is spreading far and wide. Hence, everywhere I go, I connect effortlessly to people who follow Him and His most practical and pragmatic teachings that instruct us to not abandon anything but our skepticism. He converted me, the biggest cynic around, to make me believe in life, humanity and love. I cherish my past with all its ugliness, as that is what made me gravitate towards the beauty of the present. I seldom revisit my past but when I do, it is for reflection and to learn from it, not for residency. I have given it up and moved to another place that is inhabited with genuine love and devotion. Truth, as I have learnt, is always supported by the universe. Hence, I urge my beloved Guruji to always keep me on this path.

28

Anishka and Sonakshi's Notes

Anyone can give up;
it's the easiest thing in the world to do.
But to hold it together when everyone else
would understand if you fell apart,
that's true strength.

Christopher Reeves

ANISHKA'S SENTIMENTS

Children grow up looking up to their parents; parents are very precious. No matter what wonderful things parents say to their children, if the words are not accompanied with action, children will never listen. The lives of children will be determined by how parents live their lives.

Initially it was blacker than black but that is because it was the fear of the unknown. We don't know what is lurking around the corner. Hence, the apprehension and anxiety coupled with comments from people who are also confused. No one understands as much as they would like to. Hence, they take sides, turn the issue into a competitive match and we, the children, feel that we are undoubtedly losing the game.

Society sees a divorced family as a 'broken home'. These norms keep people from thinking outside the box. When people hear about it, they pity you, feel terrible for you, and offer you their unrelenting sympathy. This is probably what makes people take longer to heal and to genuinely understand the situation that is never as bad as it is painted.

However, I began to realise that my pre-conceived notions and conditioning that I had also grown up with were inane. For a while, I even believed that I was part of that 'broken home' and that I had lost the game, and felt dreadful about it. However, when I thought about how I really felt and when I began to see how my family and I were growing from this experience, I didn't feel like a victim anymore. I observed both my parents as calmer and happier individuals. Hence, they were winning in the game of life. I'm not saying for a minute that it wasn't hard for all of us, that it was plain sailing but it was better than how it was initially portrayed. All situations cannot be painted with the same brush and my parents' divorce did not mean either of them divorcing us!

People always have problems; it's just about how you view the situation and how you choose to respond to it. You can succumb to societal reaction or see that it happened because two people were unhappy and can be happier relating to each other but not in a marriage. How you deal with this is what builds your own character. Divorce is not right or wrong but our attitudes make it so in our Indian society. Since divorce has become rampant in our culture, the average mindset needs to change too. Instead of looking down, they need to see the conviction of courage in the people involved. Divorce can be a sensible solution to an ongoing negative situation.

I had maintained a positive outlook towards my family and so did my sister. This is what made our bond stronger and eventually everything turned out great! As far as I'm concerned, we all won in the end and that's what counts as love pours into our lives from all directions.

SONAKSHI'S NOTES

Jim Carrey once said, 'I think everybody should get rich and famous and do everything they ever dreamed of, so they can see that it's not the answer.'

Since I was a little girl, I was taught that the path to happiness was simple and straightforward. It included attending a reputed university, earning a handsome salary and getting married. Basically I was taught, 'A happy life is one spent in learning, earning, and yearning.' This was the only path that would reap benefits; all others guaranteed damage. Learning and earning were seen more as duties whereas marriage was seen as the path to happiness. This belief was instilled in me by fairy tales like Cinderella where only after Prince Charming arrived did she have her 'happily-ever-after'. Life was simple: one path, one solution.

Whilst growing up, my parents seemed happy together, I never quite noticed the broken smile and sorrowful eyes. It was inconceivable to me that a couple wouldn't be happy together; they were supposed to be on the 'right' path to eternal happiness. This misconception ended the day I walked into my mother's room and saw it choked with suitcases and boxes. In between the boxes and suitcases sat my mother in total despair and despondency.

When our eyes met, we both cried endlessly. She had reached a dead end in her marriage but through the entire web of the mess, she had finally found an exit. Fear manifested in her eyes as turning away from 18 years of marriage would be an ordeal but she was ready to take the chance. Her journey should have ended when she had married my father, as Shakespeare once said:

175

'Journeys end in lovers meeting.' But she seemed to be like a mouse moving away from the cheese. I felt terribly sorry for her. I was sure that this turn of events would make both my parents eternally sad.

Apparently she wasn't the only sorry figure. 5th July 2006 marked the beginning of the many pitiful glances that came my way. Alleged well-wishers decided that I was to be the victim of their separation. I began to believe that the irrevocable damage caused by my broken home would spill over in all aspects of my life. My mother didn't have a happily-ever-after, therefore, neither could I, a pattern I apparently would not be able to break. My broken heart emanated from my broken home.

I was adrift in the jungle of life until one day, I began to see things for what they were rather than what I was led to believe. What came home to me was that I was trapped in my own conditioning. I couldn't see out of the box. This dawned on me as both my parents looked far more content and relaxed without each other than when they were together. In the passage of time, my relationship with both my parents actually improved dramatically, as both were happier individuals.

I finally realised that everybody has their own way to reach the cheese and to create their own flavour of the cheese. Whilst some find solace in marriage, others find it in work or children or in other aspects of life. Life is like a maze. It's complicated and complex but it doesn't have only one path and one answer.

29

A Final Reflection

In every desert of calamity
there is an oasis of comfort. Just look for it.

Anonymous

Divorce is synonymous with death. Death of togetherness and the
so-called eternal tie, the comfort and discomfort of a family and
all that accompanies it, including holidays, regular and irregular,
dining in, dining out, not dining at all, financial and emotional
security and insecurity, social acceptance, personal rejection and
the collapse of personal values, beliefs and cherished dreams.

It is also a new beginning. Hence, I was reborn after my
divorce and the process of birth/rebirth is never painless. The dark
and difficult are as important as the light and easy. At the time of
separation, I was dying every moment as the acrimony that came
my way was filling me with an acute sense of doubt. I pleaded for

strength to see it through. Every moment was a test and I prayed in earnest for the end to be around the corner, not in some yonder place. I underwent personal traumas that I could not relate to anyone, as my internal battle was as tumultuous as my external war, if not more. Real battles, as is often said, are fought within the soul.

Only my faith kept my body and soul together. Trust was a pre-requisite for my long-term happiness. When the truth is so clear, it cannot be suspected of any uncertainty. Although I hurt, I knew the sun would shine on me again. However, I honestly did not know how to walk through the dark to get to that light. I tried desperately to smile through my tears but mostly failed, as I was so transparent that my every emotion was drawn graphically on my face. I appeared far older than my years, with crooked frown lines on my lacklustre forehead, the smile lines around my mouth more deep and my skin tone dull, lifeless and jaded. I would stand before the mirror and rehearse a smile that would appear convincing but I could fool neither others, nor myself. My eyes revealed the sorrow and sadness that my soul felt. I wore this weathered look until I took a grip of myself, empowering myself from within and being able to walk with my head held high. My inner posture is what needed to stand tall. Eventually it did.

The truth is I never married to be divorced someday. I believed in love, marriage and its sanctity whilst I abhorred infidelity, manipulations and the abuse of its sacredness. I never believed in divorce. I still uphold my respect for the institution of marriage and I still maintain that divorce needs to be the last resort to a marital conflict unless it is ongoing and debilitating. I continue to promote the importance of marriage to both my girls, as well as a healthy comradeship with love, loyalty and laughter between two people. Although my divorce provoked the disapproval of many insular individuals, I stood my ground, as not once had I doubted the decision that was set in stone. On the contrary, I am proud of my courage in hindsight, and with time, I was able to fashion my own identity that was most liberating and rewarding.

I was strictly an old-fashioned Indian girl raised with traditional values in urban England amongst an insular Indian society more time-honoured and traditional than the Delhiites in the '80s. I grew up watching my mother dutifully and beautifully perfecting her skills in the kitchen whilst artistically sculpting the perfectly rounded chappatis (Indian bread) day in and day out to satisfy our keen Indian appetites. She was the ideal mother and wife whilst I simply dreamt of the ideal.

My being was shattered as were my hopes and aspirations and all that I stood for but then the self-deprecating attitude that was impeding my progress and the shackles of habit needed to be broken, and they indeed were. I had more than tested my tolerance in my marriage and a radical change had to be made. That came about through self-awareness, self-observation and, eventually, through self-respect.

I was broken but never once did I express it. I didn't need to. In all this, I had not severed my ties with my former in-laws. The respect was maintained, as was the cordiality between us.

Breakdowns, however, have an upside. The ordeals I went through were not insurmountable. I went into a space that was most terrifying and tumultuous. Having no choice but to face and fight my fears, I did so, sometimes with dignity and at other times, with obvious dread. When I, after years of battle, came out of this space, nothing seemed so frightening to me anymore. I was stronger than ever with more inner fortitude and conviction than anyone I ever knew. I was proud of the person I had become. Believe you me, that person was not born but made, from broken fibres, layer by layer until they shaped into a whole and wholesome entity. It took a good few years after the separation to arrive at that place of being totally comfortable in my skin. Remember, when you hit rock bottom, the only direction to go is up. I climbed slowly and steadily and sometimes unsteadily until I reached a place of personal, social and professional respect. Individual respect meant the world to me and I believe I earned it by working towards it day in and day out. For the first time in my life I was able to assert my free will.

My greatest driving force was my girls. I needed to heal my broken soul for them to love and respect me whole-heartedly. My girls often projected my fears and insecurities. Hence, it was paramount that I turned the darkness of our lives into light as soon as I possibly could. That clearly meant no longer wallowing in self-pity. I needed to pick up the pieces of my life to make good sense out of them immediately but also intelligently. The latter was not always the case! I was, as indeed I am, a highly emotional individual and during that phase, I was an emotional wreck. My journey of self-recovery began with a vengeance only after I realised the despondency and dejection in both my daughters' eyes. I was GUILTY. I had to convert the situation from hopeless to hopeful and indeed happy and fulfilling. I did this through daily prayer and my frequent visits to my Guruji's temple where I drew at His reservoir of strength and sanity. My focus on the trust factor kept my vision clear. The incapacitating guilt had to dissolve with growing awareness and consistent communication with myself and the girls. My maternal instinct for stability, predictability and safety for my girls was what took over and today I see myself as a winner.

In hindsight, I realise that I spent the first two years trying to LOOK brave, I ought to have mustered the courage to be honest about my heartache but somehow the victory of finally being able to come away from a detrimental marriage had exceeded my personal defeat of having failed my dear, innocent and shattered children. I was carrying the mountainous guilt of having let my children down in life. They deserved a healthy home with a healthy family environment which they had anyway been deprived of whilst I was in the marriage. The perennial question of them coming away from an unhealthy environment and being labelled instead as children from a broken home loomed large over me like a dark cloud that lifted as soon as I recreated a healthy home environment without a marriage. It was my challenge and belief that I could and would generate happiness for my children in a strong, hale and hearty home that I would have to single-handedly create and I eventually did.

In the passage of time, I began to develop my self-confidence, which I had lost in the deep dark forest of my internal and invisible pain. Gosh! How brilliant I had become in camouflaging my wounded soul. Today, my friends state that I gave the impression of being totally fine even immediately after walking out of the marriage on that momentous warm day of 5th July. Very slowly I began to emit a more sincere smile that gradually turned into genuine laughter and joy. I began very soon to date interesting, lively men who boosted my morale and then there would be long gaps of not dating once I felt good about myself again. I realised that I did not need a long-term relationship. Good Lord! It was a clear bold lettered 'NO NO' sign etched on my then broken heart. I needed to repair the fragments to make me whole again. Most importantly, I needed to learn to love myself and to develop a fine balance within as that is what is reflected outside too.

My friends were my salve. Without them there was no way on earth that I could have ever recuperated from my divorce or had the faith to paint! How they held me up after life knocked me down is recorded in my memory and imprinted on my soul. Although I have moved back to England, my Delhi friends are in regular touch and the closest ones have already visited me here. My Guruji has blessed me with much more than I had bargained for, and much more than I can measure in words and otherwise.

Experience teaches me that most of my reasons for staying in a demoralising marriage were irrational and illogical. Calling a spade a spade would have spared me years of unnecessary woe. Stepping back from my fears and viewing them in a more objective manner would have enabled me to walk out much earlier but then the journey through the Amazon is what prompted me to seek the higher meaning of life and I met my Guruji. His magnificence and His splendour knew no bounds as He came from celestial light and radiated it unconditionally. However, this truth can only be conceivable to those who understand the contrast to this light. My sound advice is to acknowledge a debilitating situation and reject it outright, not justify it and live in the false hope that things will get better. I do not advocate divorce but it is a healthy solution to an unhealthy marriage and although certain elements influence our decisions to stay on, we need to take a call on self-preservation. Only the wearer knows best where the shoe pinches, so no one but no one knows what happens behind closed doors except the 'wearer'.

As I see life from the other side of the fence, I acknowledge all that I have gained and all that I have lost in those 18 years. I still maintain that I have gained more than I have lost. I may have lost my youth but I have certainly gained in substance. Above all, I have gained the eternal guidance and blessings of my most revered Guruji who has more than compensated by showering me with abundant love, life and legitimate laughter.

A certain karma cuts very deep and then He comes along to heal and close the wound as if it were never there.

30

For My Daughters

Feel it, deal with it
and trust the divine to heal it.

Anonymous

Today, I have separated myself from the negative aspects of my
past. Time will play its part in fading the memories into the
unreachable distance. I have moved out of the shadows and I now
walk into light. I have won many battles and learnt many lessons.
The greatest one that I impart to my daughters is the lesson of
self-love. Love and respect yourselves and the world will mirror
that back to you along with a genuinely admiring smile. Be strong
but sensitive; be courageous but compassionate. When you feel
complete within yourself, your partner will compliment who you
are. Never lose your female identity and individuality and always
see the world through a positive window, as it is full of goodness
and grace. Maintain inner balance and forbid anyone to challenge

your personal liberty and dignity. Believe and embrace Divinity for it will see you through the rough to make you tough and to bring about the smooth. Of course, I do go through pangs of regret for taking 18 years to break free but I focus on all that I have achieved during that time with the two of you, Anishka and Sonakshi. If you are the owner of your smile, then no one can make you cry.

To those who are perhaps going through the rough journey of a divorce and recovery, I strongly suggest you embark on a spiritual journey and ensure many other travellers walk the path too. There is no greater joy than to reach out to other passersby. Once we start interacting with others, we realise that human hurt is the same everywhere. The problems are the same everywhere and the solutions too are universal. The enormity of strength and wisdom we derive from the divine cannot be undermined. For me, the earthy, natural surroundings of Guruji's temple with the promise of real sustaining love and joy in the air, promoted my inner peace, serenity and sanity! Whilst I went from strength to strength in my journey, I also became approachable for other disciples who needed reassurance and evidence of Guruji's unending powers! Imparting my experiences of faith reaffirmed my own too, as in moments of despair, there is always a nagging doubt about His presence in my life. I needed proof *all the time!!* It's almost as if my brain forgets and then it needs a miracle for it to refresh my memory. How exhausting for Guruji as I still don't let Him be! There is an indefinable feeling of satisfaction in knocking on His door every millisecond of my life!

'Challenges make life interesting, however, overcoming them is what makes life meaningful,' says Joshua J Marine. Alongside, there are three practical things to do to ease the journey:

PHYSICAL: Join a gym or any pleasurable form of dance or fun physical activity.

EMOTIONAL: Maintain a diary (it may not win the Booker Prize but it will make you feel good) and take up meditation and yoga.
LINGUISTIC: Take up a language and become a prolific reader.

D	Determination	Forge ahead with renewed tenacity.
I	Introspection	Improve your inner life through prayer/ meditation/yoga.
V	Vitality	Engage in various activities to stimulate the mind and body.
O	Openness	Share your life with friends and be forward thinking.
R	Resilience	Bounce back to the best version of yourself.
C	Courage	Have the stand-alone spirit in all situations.
E	Exercise	Join gym/dance/yoga/ classes and walk in the open.

ENCOURAGEMENT FOR WOMEN

Someone will always be prettier, smarter, richer, better and have more than you. Just let it go. Take care of yourself. Love yourself and your circumstances. The prettiest, slimmest woman in the world may have sadness in her heart. The most highly favoured woman in your office may not be able to have children. The richest woman you know may have the car, the house and the clothes but may be very lonely. So love who you are right now. Tell yourself, 'I am too blessed to be stressed.' Be well. Be happy. Be blessed.

Epilogue

I now walk through life, the best I know
I follow others through the dark patches where I cannot see
And shed light onto those who fall behind.

Je ne regrette rien
Ni le bien ni le mauvais

I regret nothing
Neither the good nor the bad

Om Namah Shivay Shivji Sada Sahay
Om Namah Shivay Guruji Sada Sahay